Lun*na Menoh

A Ring Around The Collar

TamTam Books

First published by TamTam Books, 2014
Printed in Japan

TamTam Books edited and published by Tosh Berman
Art Direction & Design by Ueno★ Amore★Hirosuke
Lun*na Menoh On Duty blog: www.lunnamenoh.blogspot.com

ISBN: 978-0-9852724-1-8
Distributed by ARTBOOK/D.A.P.
155 6th Avenue, 2nd Floor
New York, NY 10013 www.artbook.com
www.tamtambooks.com
www.tamtambooks-tosh.blogspot.com

Contents

Introduction

Lun*na Menoh's Dirty Laundry

Leslie Dick

We order our world through sets of opposed ideas: work/play, serious/funny, pain/pleasure, etc. We count on artists to undo these oppositions, to cut them loose. Turning such systems inside out, we discover the bright lining of absurdity concealed within. Order is always vulnerable to such reversals, in which the hilarity of work, the pleasure of obsession, and the sharp pain of our designated roles and routines become suddenly, undeniably apparent. Even something as ordinary, as everyday, as a dirty shirt collar can be deployed in this struggle against received ideas, and something as familiar and seemingly insignificant as a collar can become a wedge, driven into an invisible crack in the system, breaking it open.

Lun*na Menoh's fourteen year project takes the dirty shirt collar and puts it through a series of permutations, thereby inviting us to consider its meanings, to find out its mode of operation and its function. To bring the lowly shirt collar to our attention is a kind of reversal in itself, an inside out, as the part of the collar that is marked by the body – the sweaty band that rests against the skin of the neck – tends to be invisible. Dirty laundry is not supposed to be aired in public. The "stubborn" stains remaining on the inner lining of the collar stand in for the body in all sorts of ways – the stubborn body, whose demands we can never completely ignore or transcend; the shameful body, whose fluids leave marks that should never be seen; the abject body, which is found at the border, an indeterminate point between subject and object. The collar traces a boundary line between public and private, conceal and reveal, mapping a space that is always negotiable in fashion, always eroticized, always a site of fascination and curiosity. Situated at the line where head and body merge, or emerge, the collar marks the place where clothing begins.

What is a collar? It's something the ubiquitous T-shirt lacks. It can be detachable, but generally speaking it is a built-in component of a man's dress shirt, with a curved band that stands up against the neck and a flat section which folds over the band, making a tunnel for the tie around the neck. Historically shirts derive from the undergarments people wore beneath their more public, more permanent clothing. Made out of linen, and later cotton, following the commercial production of cheap cotton by slaves in the United States and factory workers in the north of England, these shirts and shifts were easy to wash. They were also relatively cheap, so for example a Victorian governess might own one or two dresses (wool, possibly silk for special occasions) and these would never be washed, only brushed and aired to clean them. Beneath these dresses she would wear shifts and petticoats, chemises and pantaloons, cotton garments that could lie against the skin, pick up the marks and stains of the body, and withstand the rigors of regular laundering: scrubbed in near boiling water, rinsed clear, and dried in the sun and open air.

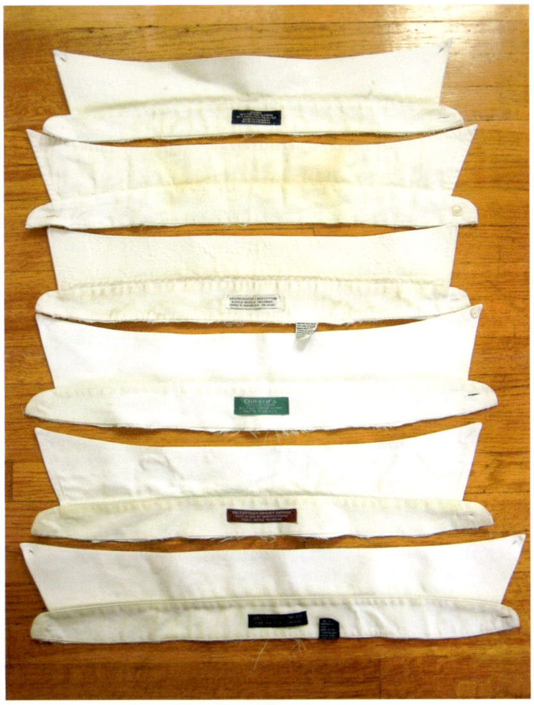

In other words, the white dress shirt, classically worn with the gentleman's three-piece suit, is historically connected to a set of garments that are traditionally invisible, except in tiny glimpses, the edge of a cuff, the collar. These edges are eroticized, as all underwear evokes the memory of a naked body in all its languor and excess. And everything we wear has the potential to speak our social status, not only our cultural capital (how to dress well, or appropriately, or beautifully) but also our actual capital. A clean shirt, perfectly white and ironed, announces every day that I have the wherewithal to pay someone (the laundress) to produce such a thing, through her skill and her labor. A clean shirt, fresh every day, declares me to be a member of the bourgeois workforce, sufficient, officiont, offoctivo, and modern.

The laundry, where we drop off our shirts and pick them up, stiff and bright in their boxes, folded around their cardboard supports, this convenient laundry is a phenomenon of the city, where "collective servants" meet our needs. While wealthy people once employed full-time cooks, gardeners, chauffeurs, and live-in maids, the 20th century city dweller enjoyed restaurants, public parks, taxis, and a daily, the British term for a domestic cleaner, usually a woman, who came to the house once or twice a week, and worked for a number of people on a daily basis. The convenience of the professional laundry, and the absolute requirement of a perfectly pressed, sparkling white shirt, was undeniable.

The specter of the recalcitrant dirty collar, its ring refusing to budge, is a post- World War II phenomenon. It was not only a product of advertising, as large corporations like Procter & Gamble and Unilever plotted with their advertising gurus to produce social anxieties in order to sell more detergent and bleach. It was also a product of the expulsion of women from the war-time work force: with peace, economic logic dictated that women had to go home, ceding their new-found independence and autonomy to the soldiers returning from World War II. Women were not only obliged to give up their jobs in order to have children and an apparently stable home, they were often lured out of the city, that domain of the collective servant, into the suburbs, in search of an idealized vision of family life. It was typically in suburbia that the otherwise unemployed housewife (entirely financially dependent on her husband) became the cook, the cleaner, the chauffeur, the gardener, the nanny, and not least, the laundress. It became a matter of personal pride for her to send her husband out into the world wearing a perfectly clean shirt. She lived in a strange isolation, far from an extended family, without the wives' tales and lore about housework and laundry that might instruct or support her in her struggle. In no time, the language of corporate advertisers took the opportunity to prey on her solitude, proposing the dirty collar as an enemy that must be vanquished. Failure was unthinkable, even if the only person who ever contemplated that stained inner band, the notorious ring around the collar, was the woman washing and ironing the shirt. It was a battle against shame.

The clean white shirt declares our commitment to the system. The housewife who doesn't care about it is clearly having a nervous breakdown and might stop feeding her children next. On the other hand, the housewife who appears in the detergent advertisements is also having a nervous breakdown, as she personifies the stain on the collar as her very own enemy, in a paranoiac projection that conveys her isolation and her vulnerability. (In the Wisk TV commercial, indelibly imprinted on the psyches of women and children everywhere, the ironed shirts, placed carefully in a suitcase, taunt the housewife with their malicious chant: "Ring around the collar!") As housewives, we are either slovenly or obsessive/compulsive. It's a no-win situation.

Lun*na Menoh offers us a third position: "The ring around the collar is our friend." And with this statement, all the ideological structures start to come apart, falling like a house of cards. If the *ring around the collar* is not the enemy, does that mean the body is not shameful? That what once remained hidden, obliterated by bleach, is beautiful ? That the discarded white shirts, with their indelible stains, have something more to say ?

Lun*na Menoh detached the collars from hundreds of used white shirts, each retaining its stains and its sewn-in label, and using the classic Situationist strategy of *détournement*, she re-functioned them, setting them to operate in another context, within another framework of ideas. The detour in *détournement* is critical: when we encounter the collars in a new context, the old set of ideas associated with these objects remains as an echo, or shadow, recalling the shame and the struggle from before. The repudiation of the body implicit in the battle against the *ring around the collar* is an undercurrent, or subtext, to this work. And the work is haunted by the ghostly figure of the mad, smiling housewife, personified in photographs of Lun*na Menoh herself, locked in her endless daily battle against dirt, with her faithful allies by her side: her washing machine, her detergent, and her bleach. In undoing this narrative, the intensity and absurdity of the housewife's role is implicitly questioned, as is the task of the housewife/mother to subjugate and master all evidence of bodily excess. She's saving the world, and her only helpers are inanimate, recruited from the supermarket shelves, peopling her isolation with promises of loyalty and sheer determination to the end of time. We will always be here for you, Tide, Wisk, and Clorox proclaim. You can count on us.

Lun*na Menoh's work doesn't address these questions directly: her work sidesteps history and politics, letting the collars do the

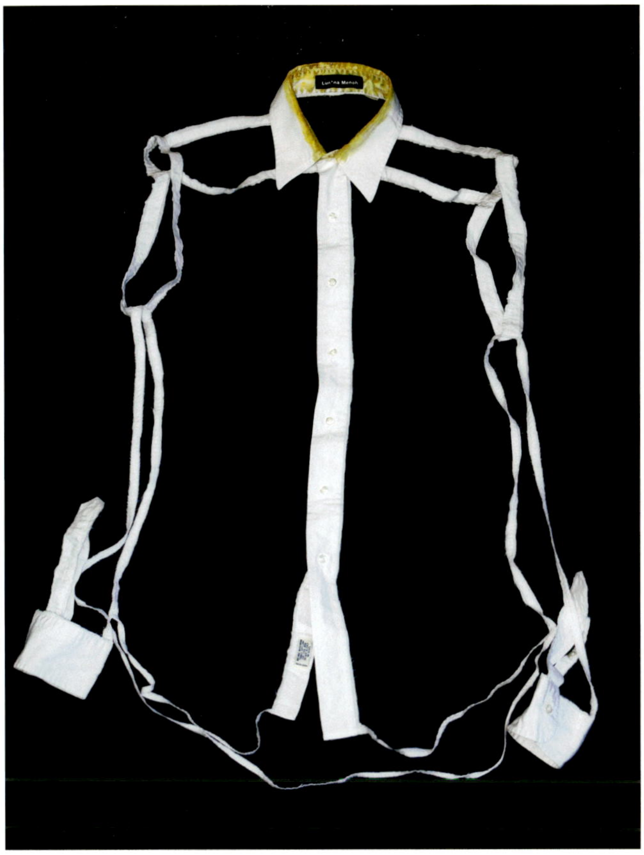 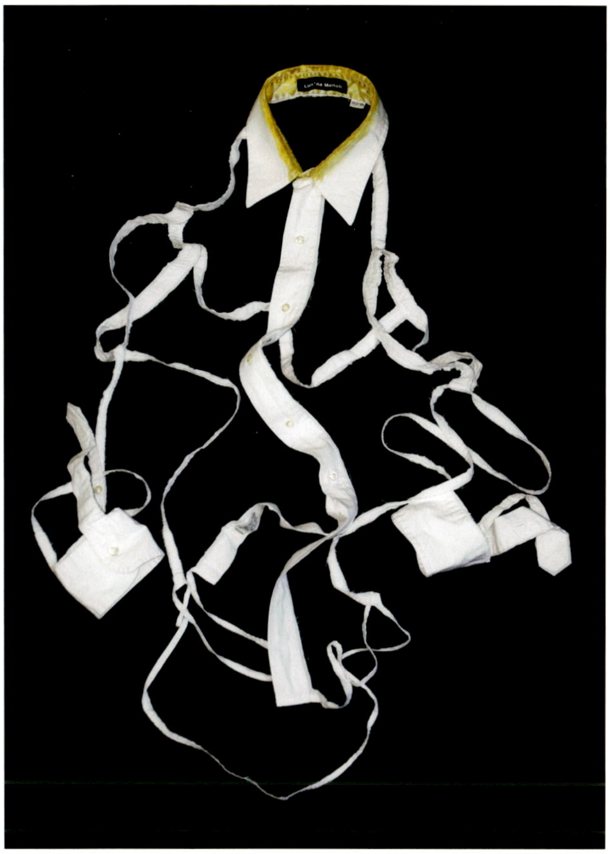

talking. Nevertheless, her photographs of the housewife, posed in her apron as if in an advertisement, speak of the fantasy space of the inhabitants of the 20th century suburban home, where every speck of dirt comes to life, in a terrifying accusation, and the task of cleaning up every day is presented as an adventure, with the housewife/mom the hero. It goes without saying that this figure, the housewife/mom, no longer exists. For some time now, the earned income of two working adults has been required to maintain a middle class home, and in many contexts, it is the woman of the family who is more able to find and keep a job. Yet we continue to be haunted by the archetypal housewife, as we slide along a spectrum of shame (frozen pizza) and pride (home baked cookies), regarding our housekeeping failures and successes from the perspective of an internalized, hypercritical judge. The vision of the crazed, smiling housewife is a hyperbolic dream version of our contemporary lives and, like an ineradicable stain, she doesn't go away.

In 1969, Mierle Laderman Ukeles presented the Maintenance Art Manifesto, in which she acknowledged the distinction between productive work (eg. making things in a factory, a repetitive task that ends with a product) and maintenance work (eg. cleaning the bathroom, a task that must be repeated, indefinitely, as the product, a clean bathroom, vanishes immediately). Ukeles noted the gender designations that traditionally belong to each category of labor, and she noted the ways in which conceptual artists were themselves questioning the idea that art itself must fall into the first, "productive" category. Concluding that much contemporary art was "maintenance"-oriented, she proceeded to declare all the maintenance work she did every day to be her art practice. There would be no product, or rather, what would be produced would be the ongoing operations of everyday life. The question of how to get paid for her artwork/housework remained unanswered, allowing space for questioning a system where artists often go unpaid, as their labor is regarded as somehow satisfying in itself – much like the housewife's labor. If an artist is like a housewife, does that make him less

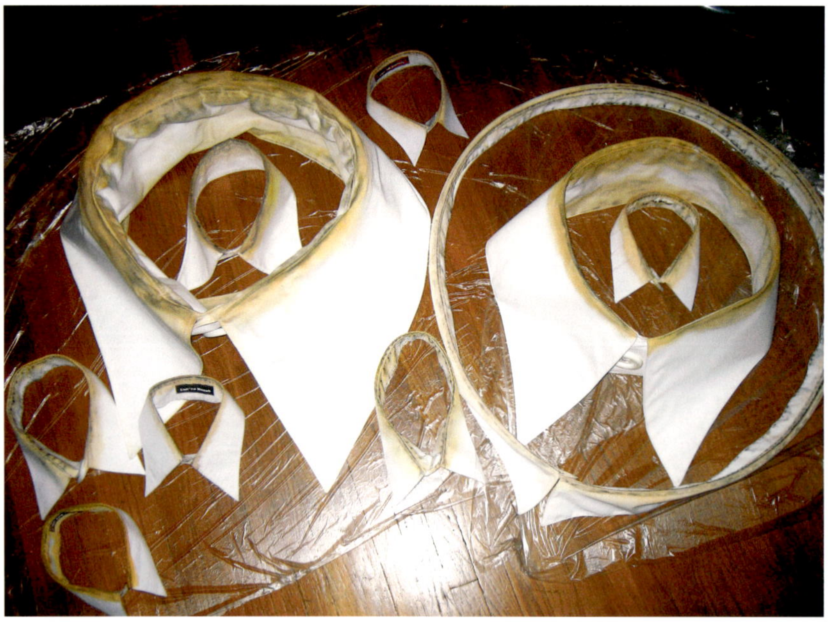

sexy, less powerful, less of a genius? Or does he suddenly seem even crazier? The house of cards comes tumbling down.

If the mad housewife and the mad artist are the same person, what they have in common is their madness, itself perhaps an appropriate response to the contradictions of the feminine predicament. As the Italian feminists Rivolta Femminile argued in 1968, for women and mothers to demand recognition (or indeed payment) for their housework and childcare exposes them to the charge of being unloving, and therefore unlovable. To refuse to care is to become unwomanly, dissolving our hard-won femininity. If the price of gender stability is an obsession with clean collars, so be it. Madness is the only logical response.

Unlike Mierle Laderman Ukeles, Lun*na Menoh does not retrieve domestic work for art; on the contrary, she rejects the task of stain eradication and celebrates the overlooked, the discarded, the abject shirt collar itself. Inadvertent sweat stains are recognized as action paintings, unconscious mark-making that results from an unmediated encounter between skin and fabric. The shirt is worn to work, nine to five, five days a week, and the shadowy ring resonates with a quotidian performance of compliance and uniformity. Instead of the housewife struggling to erase these marks of the passage of time, the working body that left the stains is recognized. "Toil was never so beautiful," Lun*na Menoh's work declares. The unconscious, miniature stain paintings that remain on the collar call into question a value system that recognizes Jackson Pollock's embodied gestures as high art, while ignoring the previously unseen aesthetic contributions of the office worker and the "salary man." In a structural reversal, Lun*na Menoh reveals what had before been hidden and implicitly asks why.

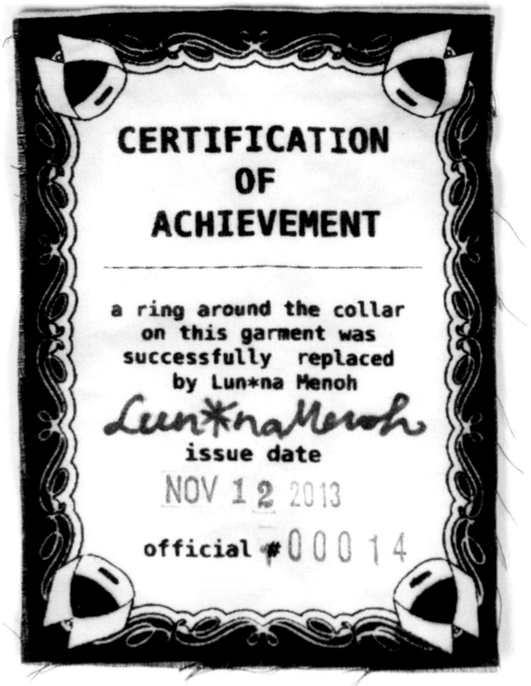

In their sewn-in labels, each collar bears witness to a history and geography of manufacture, as well as to the cultural values conveyed by brands and designer names. (One piece, the punk kilt, is constructed from collars manufactured in many places: Guatemala, United States, Hong Kong, Korea, Malaysia, China, Honduras.) Often the designer label that purports to connect the shirt to Paris or London is actually manufactured out of polyester and cotton in a Latin American or Asian country. The logic of a globalized late capitalism is encapsulated in these miniature histories, where the promise of power and style offered by the label is instantly dissolved in the reality of international sweatshops and cheap transportation on container ships.

The shirt collar has not changed its design in over one hundred years, for a number of reasons. Arguably it performs its function perfectly, which is to hold the shirt close against the neck, both retaining body heat and affording the tie, that last vestige of decoration in traditional male dress, a stable foundation. It also allows for the moment of relaxation, when the tie's knot is pulled open and the collar button is undone, at last, thus signifying a relaxation of formality. This gesture occurs in the bar after work, or perhaps it marks the moment at the end of the working day when the salary man comes home, and his smiling wife hands him a martini as reward for his bravery in facing the world. The collar serves both to articulate a formal, public persona, and to undo that presentation, to map the space of leisure and relaxation.

The collar frames the face and makes us aware of the neck, that highly erotic space that connects my speaking self to my body, the place where my voice originates, where language and the body coincide. The loosened collar is the first point of access to the body, inviting perhaps a further unbuttoning: a reprieve from repression. Men's suits, and the shirts, shoes, and accessories they require,

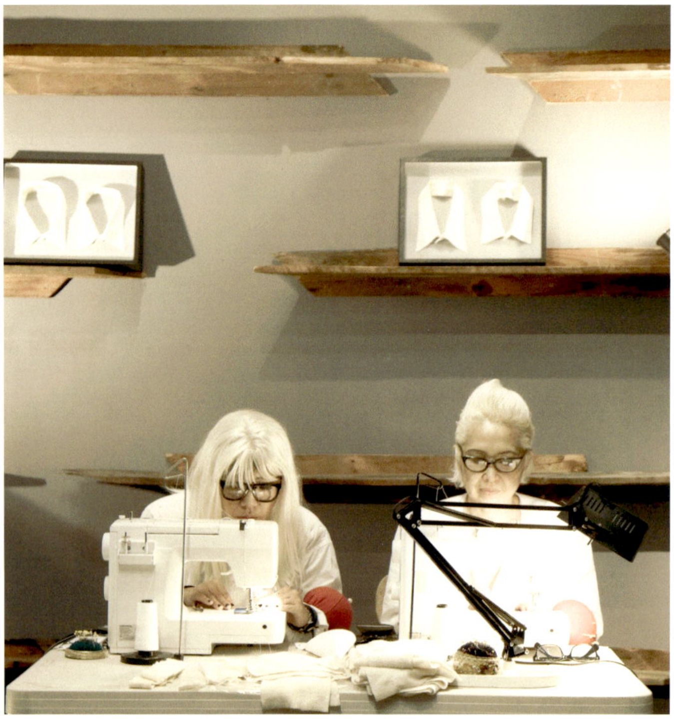

are fundamentally unchanged partly because they are so efficient. Yet they are also sites of erotic articulation, producing a vocabulary of layers and buttons and ties and belts that opens the body to language and its pleasurable permutations. The collar is the boundary where the clothed body begins, and as such it is the site of fantasy as well as the last place, the last moment, where the insistent body leaves its traces. Perhaps we are obliged to eradicate the ring around the collar, in case it climbs higher, moving up the neck, to contaminate our minds.

Lun*na Menoh's work takes the endlessly washed yet eternally stained collars and sews them into new forms: a wedding dress, a boombox, a Hermès Kelly bag, a motorcycle jacket. What was previously hidden and overlooked becomes a covering, like a slipcover, for different objects, in a move that shifts the stains from concealment to display. Furniture is dressed in abandoned collars, sewn into a monochromatic patchwork of failed white. The collars have a smell that cannot be eradicated, and this grounds their stains in a body history that cannot be forgotten. Lun*na Menoh's work celebrates something that's dirty, merely because it's dirty. And the everyday connotation of *dirty* with *sexy* is precisely where the work sits, looking out at us as if to say, is dirty bad? Is sexy bad? Are bodies bad? Then I'm bad, too. And you?

There's a profound hilarity in the work, and at the same time a deep seriousness, evidenced by the years of production and the many forms the work takes. Lun*na Menoh's paintings of solitary collars, each announcing its provenance through the meticulous language of its sewn-in label, propose a fundamental connection between stains and painting. Her paintings of phantom pop stars, evoked by their characteristic collars, demonstrate the framing of the absent face, the work the collar does. Her garments made out of recycled collars are perfectly tailored, invoking the immutable fashion form while simultaneously subverting it. We are haunted by these archetypal forms – the wedding dress, the kilt, or the Kelly handbag. Re-making them out of discards performs a translation, in which the fashion archetype or ideal becomes materialized through an encounter with an insistent yet rejected, repudiated body.

The stained shirt collars stand in for everything society demands of us: nine-to-five discipline, the laundry wars fought in isolation and despair, the suppression of an excessive, smelly body. When our aspirations take form, in a wedding dress for example, all of that anguish is left behind, designated as beneath contempt. Lun*na Menoh's *ring around the collar* work deconstructs these oppositions, insisting that the body, that dirty thing, be part of the equation. She reminds us that we are nothing without that dirty thing, and all our ideals and aspirations are grounded in and made out of sweat, blood, and tears. There's a wild pleasure embodied in these hybrid forms, where the overlooked and the rejected take center stage, becoming the material that allows these ideals to exist. Deep in the absurdity, the irony, and the delight is a radical operation that overturns preconceptions and turns value systems inside out, as the imaginary housewife who doesn't care about the *ring around the collar* turns out to care very much, remembering the absent bodies that left these marks behind.

Leslie Dick has taught in the Art Program at CalArts since 1992. She is a writer of two novels, *Without Falling* (1987) and *Kicking* (1992), and a collection of short stories, *The Skull of Charlotte Corday* (1995). Her writing has appeared in various magazines, art catalogues, and anthologies, and she writes regularly for *X-TRA*, a quarterly journal of contemporary art, whose editorial board she joined in 2011. She collaborated with artist Martin Kersels on a video, *Ripcord* (2008), and in 2010, she presented a "multi-media performance" of Jacques Lacan's essay on the mirror stage at the Whitney Museum in New York. She is currently Visiting Critic in Sculpture at Yale University.

OAKTON
the fitted shirt
single needle tailoring
65%polyester, 35%cotton
tailored in Korea
machine wash warm
gentle cycle white-bleach
when needed
color/stripes
only non-chlorine bleach when needed
tumble dry- medium remove promptly
if pressed use warm iron

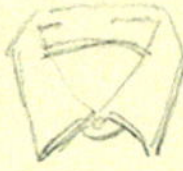

LINEAR DIMENSIONS
70%polyester-30%cotton
single needle tailoring
tailored in Korea
machine wash warm
gentle cycle, tumble dry
remove promptly cool iron

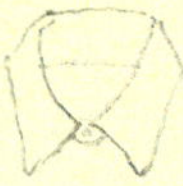

OAKTON
60%cotton-40%polyester
assembled in Costa Rica

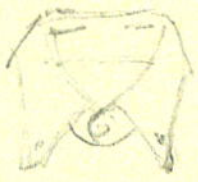

GRANTS
men's wear
permanent press
50% polyester-50%cotton
machine wash warm
tumble dry

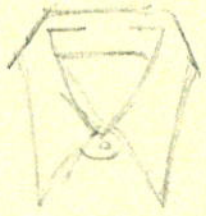

STEP WALK

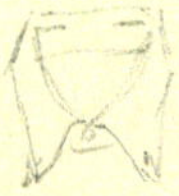

ARNIE II
100%cotton pinpoint oxford
single needle tailoring
made in U.S.A.

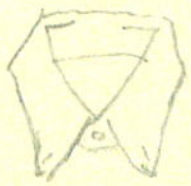

JC PENNY
all cotton easy care
single needle tailoring
machine wash
no chlorine bleach
tumble dry medium setting
remove promptly
if pressed use steam iron

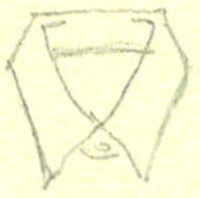

JARROD'S
100%cotton
made in Malaysia
machine wash warm
tumble dry low
only non-chlorine bleach
when needed
steam iron medium

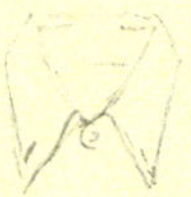

STAFFORD
60%cotton-40%polyester
single needle tailoring
made in U.S.A.
machine wash warm
tumble dry low
non-chlorine bleach
only when needed
remove promptly warm
iron for touch up

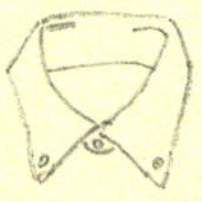

ALFANI
single needle tailoring
55%cotton-45%polyester
made in El Salvador
machine wash warm
setting tumble dry low
press with steam iron
use only non-chlorine bleach
when needed

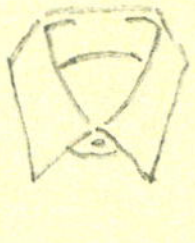

ADOLFO
extra full body
55%cotton-45%polyester
imported fabric
tailored in U.S.A.
machine wash in warm water
gentle cycle, tumble dry medium
remove promptly
do not bleach. cool iron if desired
wash dark colors separately

HENNESSY BY VAN HEUSEN
single needle tailoring
65%polyester, 35%cotton
tailored in China

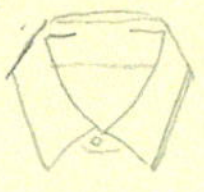

MARQUIS
65%polyester-35% cotton
made in Korea
machine wash warm
tumble dry low
use no bleach

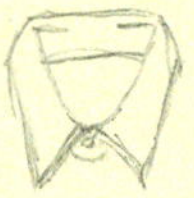

KETCH
single needle tailoring
65%polyester 35%cotton
made in Korea
machine wash warm
with like colors
gentle cycle
tumble dry low
remove promptly
cool iron if desired
only non-chlorine bleach
when needed

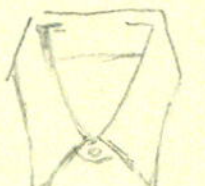

PERRY ELLIS PORTFOLIO
100%cotton
made in U.S.A. of imported fabric
machine wash warm
dark colors separately
tumble dry low press damp
only non-chlorine bleach
when needed

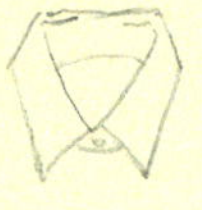

SEARS
men's store
perma-prest
65%cotton 35%polyester
made in Korea

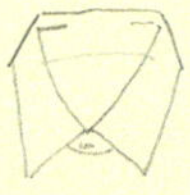

WRANGLER
exec by red kap
machine wash
made in U.S.A.

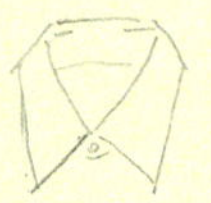

CALVIN KLEIN
made in Indonesia
100%cotton
machine wash warm
tumble dry warm
warm iron
no chlorine bleach
can be professionally dry cleaned

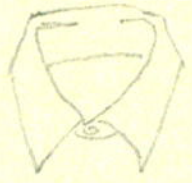

CICERO BEVERLY HILLS
fine combed cotton
fin cotton peigne
single needle
100%cotton
made in Canada
machine wash, warm iron
no chlorine bleach

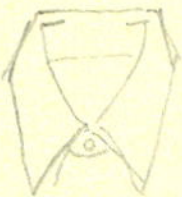

GEOFFREY BEENE
55%cotton-45%polyester
made in Honduras
machine wash warm
tumble dry-cool iron
only non-chlorine bleach
when needed

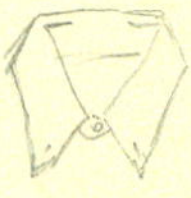

STANLEY BLACKER
single needle tailoring
55%cotton-45%polyester
made in Guatemala
machine wash warm
tumble dry low heat
no bleach
iron if necessary

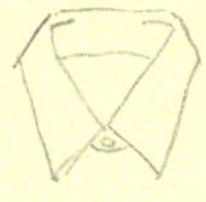

GEOFFREY BEENE
cotton
100%cotton
made in U.S.A. of imported fabric
machine wash warm
gentle cycle tumble dry
remove promptly steam iron
whites bleachable colors
only non-chlorine bleach when needed

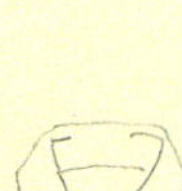

STAFFORD
pinpoint oxford
80%cotton 20%polyester
assembled in Honduras
machine wash- warm gentle cycle
do not bleach
tumble dry- medium
remove promptly
steam iron

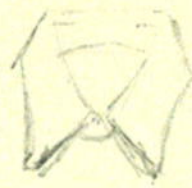

DON JUAN
New York U.S.A.
60%cotton 40%polyester
machine wash
warm tumble dry
remove promptly

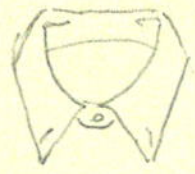

JS.A.BANK
executive collection
imported pinpoint oxford
made in Singapore
100% cotton
machine wash
tumble dry low
bleach white only
use non-chlorine bleach
iron at warm setting

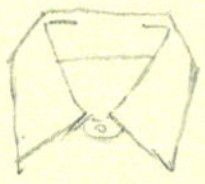

LEVI'S
modern authentics
100%cotton
made in Indonesia
machine wash warm
tumble dry
hot iron if needed

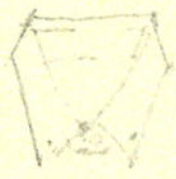

VITTORIO REX
made in Italy
single needle tailoring
70%cotton, 30%polyester
machine wash warm,
tumble dry. use only non-chlorine
bleach when needed.
damp ironing required.

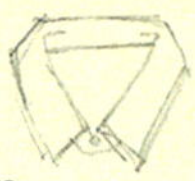

TOWN CRAFT
65%polyester, 35%cotton
made in Taiwan
machine wash
tumble dry
only non-chlorine bleach
when needed
warm iron as needed

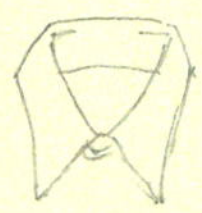

CLASSIC FASHIONS BY VAN HEUSEN
single needle tailoring
65%polyester-35%cotton
made in Indonesia

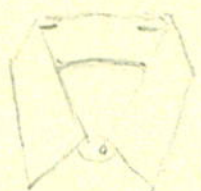

PURITAN
wrinkle free
inarrugable
65%polyester 35%cotton
made in U.S.A. of imported fabric
machine wash warm setting

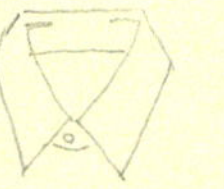

THE ARROW COMPANY
est 1851
wrinkle free oxford
60%cotton-40%polyester
made in Costa Rica
wash dark colors separately
machine wash warm
gentle cycle
only non-chlorine bleach
when needed
tumble dry on cottons setting/medium
remove promptly
if pressed use warm iron

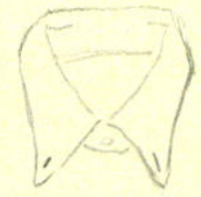

BROOKS BROTHERS
all cotton
machine wash or
commercially laundered
neutral ph only
non-chlorine bleach
tailored in Honduras

PIERRE CARDIN
100%cotton
tailored in Burma
machine wash warm
wash darks separately
use only non-chlorine bleach
when needed tumble dry low
remove promptly cool iron

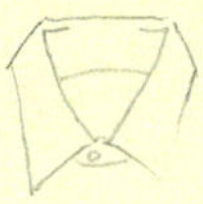

NORDSTROM
classic
finest imported 2x2
100%cotton pin point
made in Singapore
machine wash warm
gentle cycle
tumble or drip dry
use no bleach

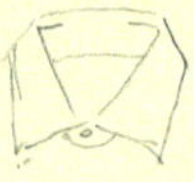

L.L.BEAN
Freeport, Maine
made in U.S.A.
60%cotton 40%polyester
single needle tailoring

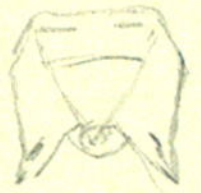

BUNCE BROTHERS
Cleveland
R.&O.Hawick
imported fabric
made in America
100%cotton
machine wash warm
tumble dry med.
warm iron only
non-chlorine bleach
when needed

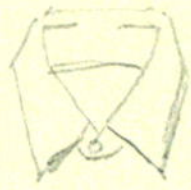

YVES SAINT LAURENT
65%polyester 35%cotton
made in Taiwan
fabrique a Taiwan
machine wash warm-gentle cycle
tumble dry low cool iron
only non-chlorine bleach-when needed

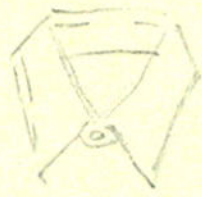

PRIORITIES BY VAN HEUSEN
single needle tailoring
60%cotton-40%polyester
made in U.S.A.
machine wash warm
gentle cycle tumble dry
remove promptly
cool iron
white- bleachable colors-
only non-chlorine bleach
when needed

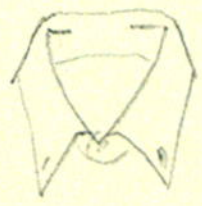

SURREY
single needle tailoring
65%polyester 35%cotton
made in Korea
machine wash warm
tumble dry medium
cool iron, if required on colors-
only non-chlorine bleach when needed

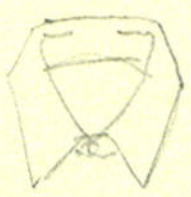

HENRI VALDISE'
65%polyester 35%cotton
made in Korea
machine wash warm
tumble dry low
do not bleach
warm iron as needed

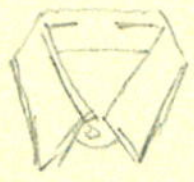

ROYAL PIERRE CARDIN

CLUB ROOM
pin point oxford
single needle
made in Singapore
100%cotton
machine wash warm setting
tumble dry low
press with steam iron
use only non-chlorine bleach
when needed

The Collar in the Box

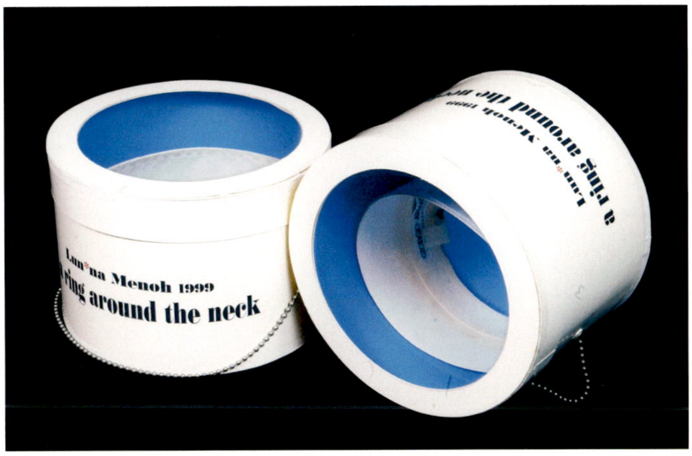

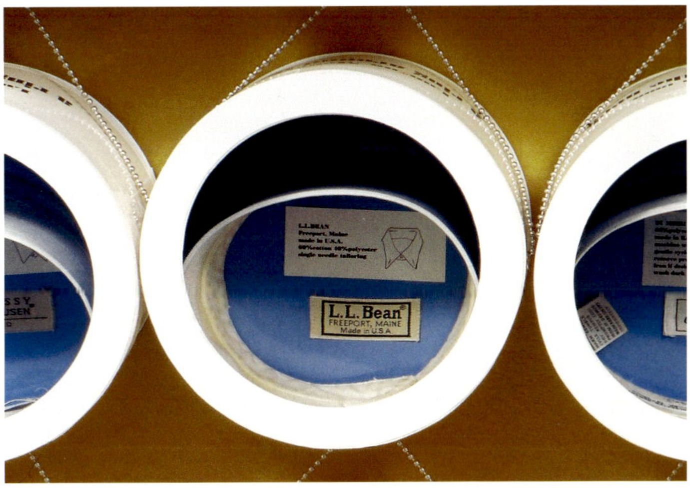

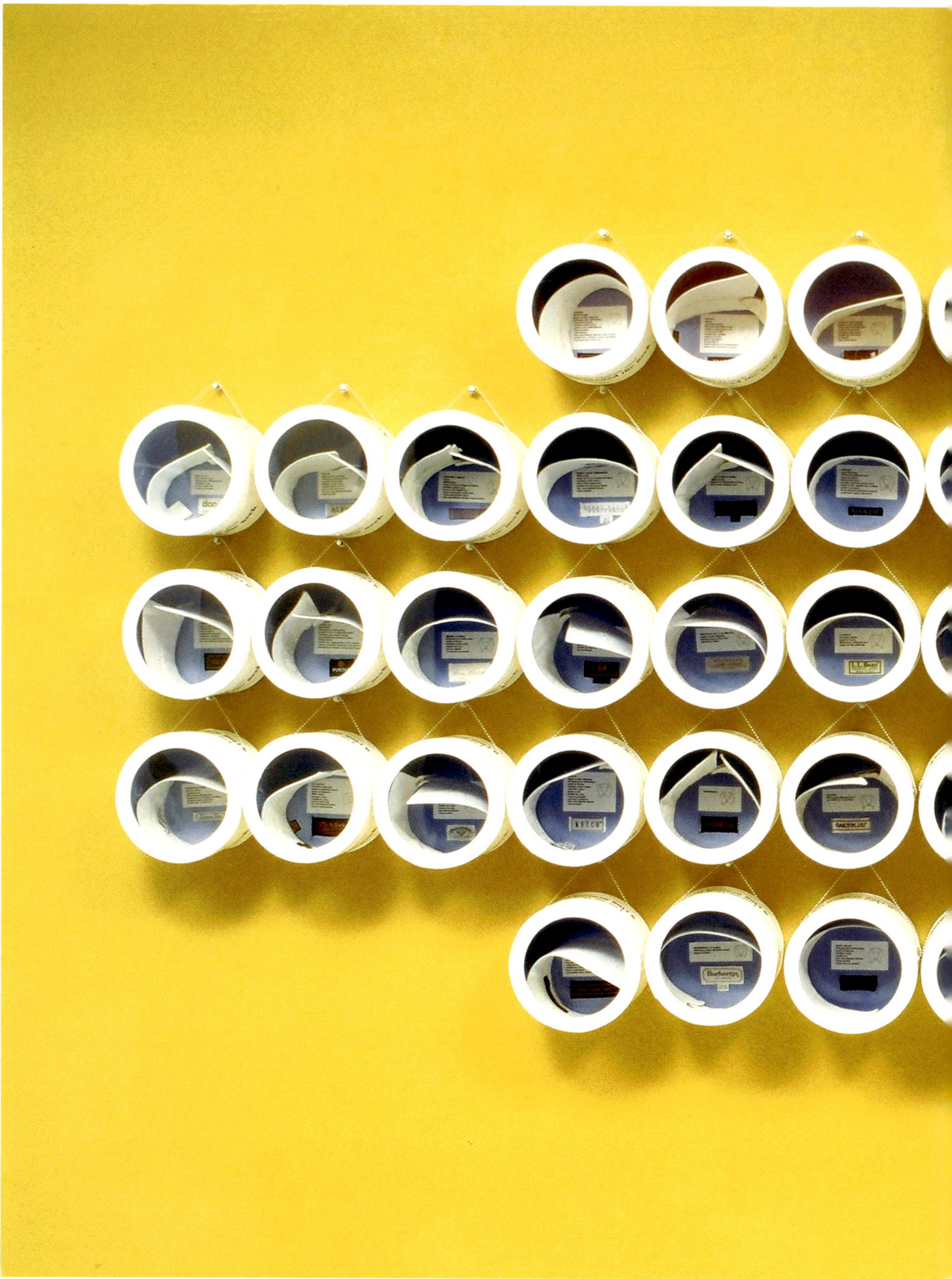

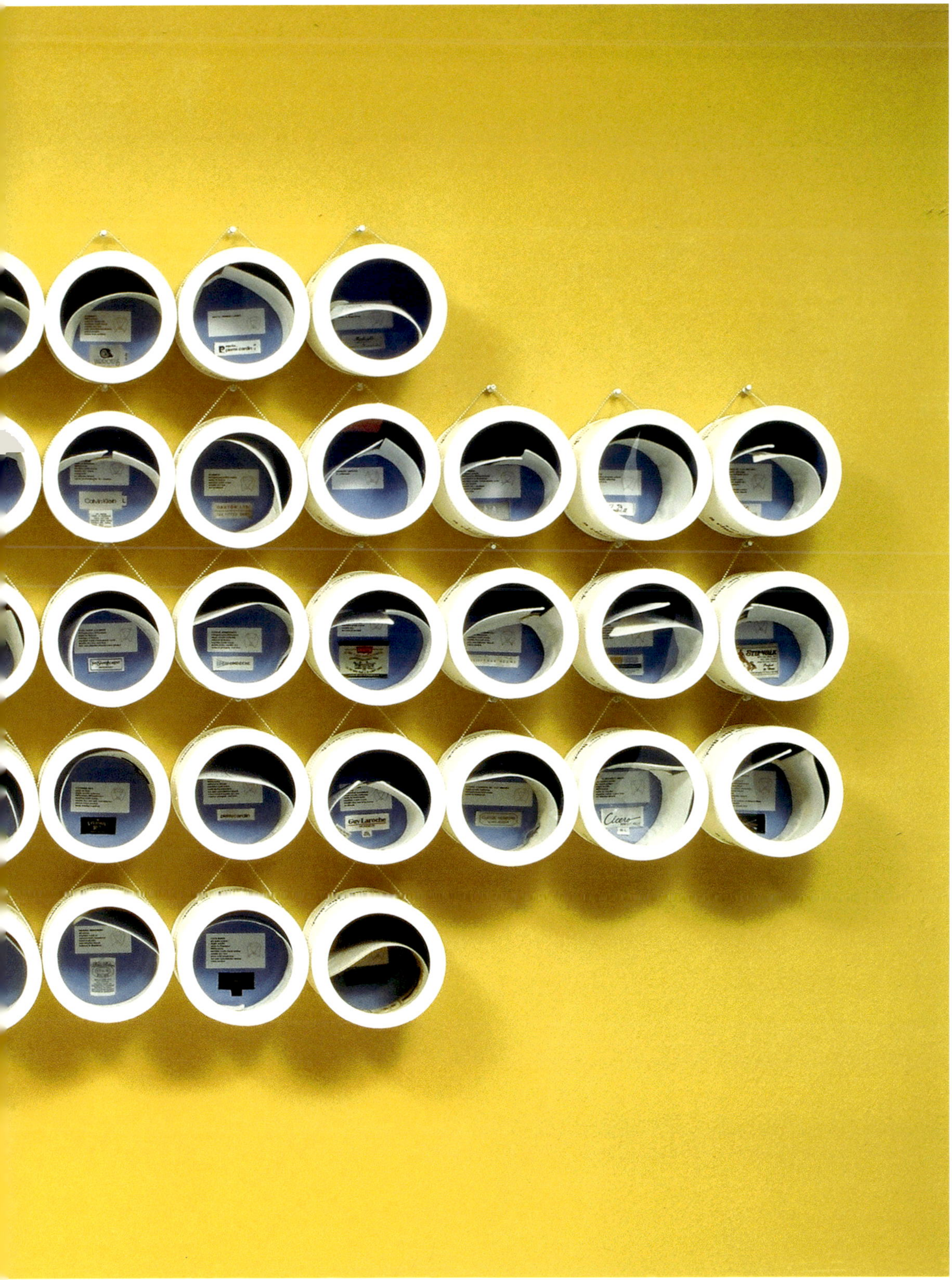

Dirty Collar Dresses

fashion show 2001

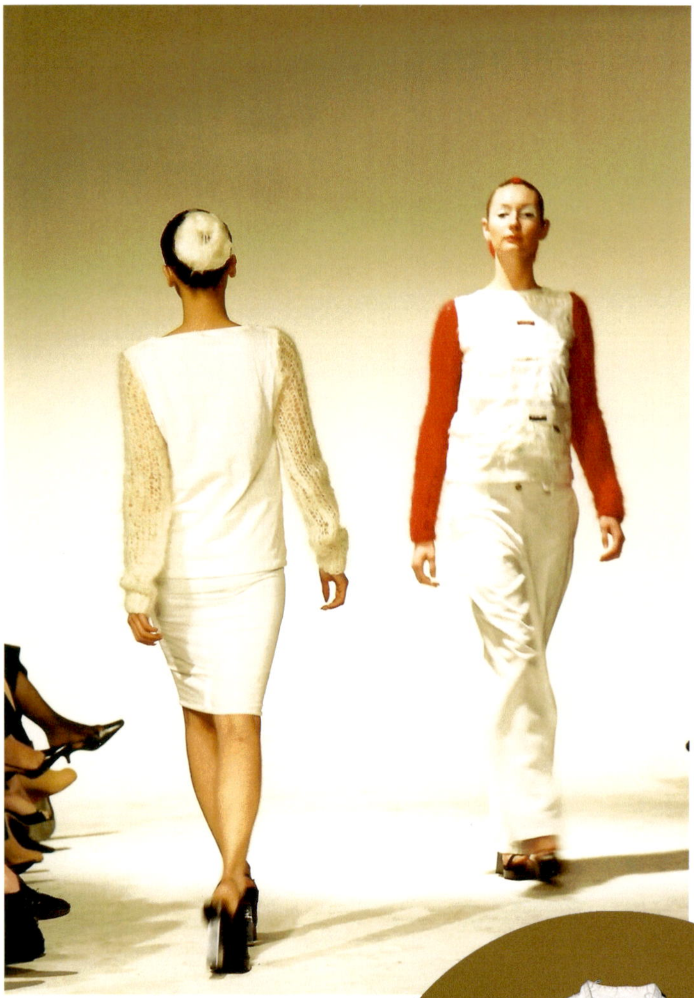

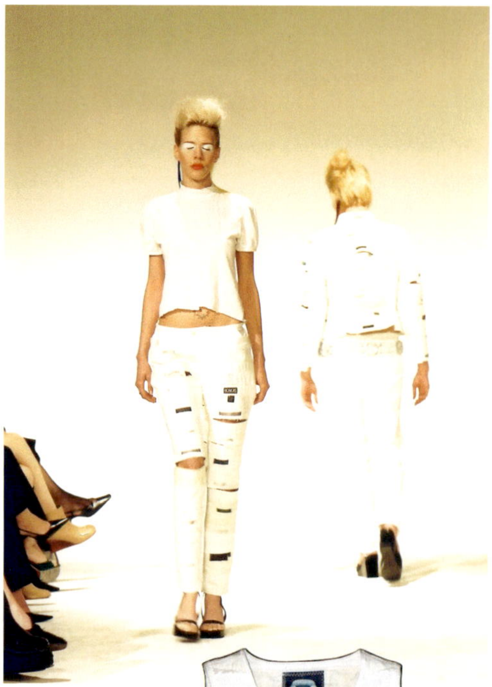

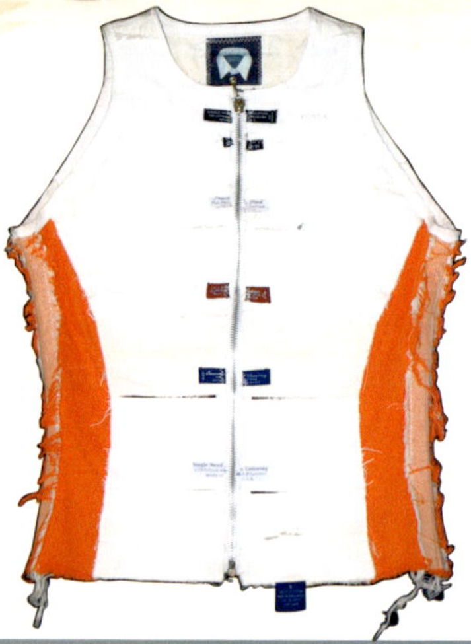

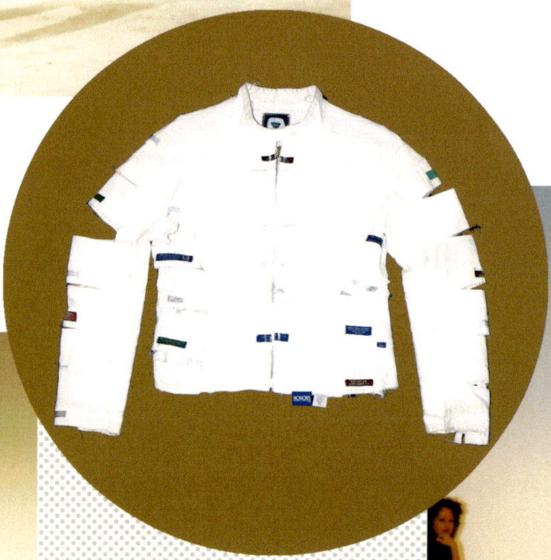

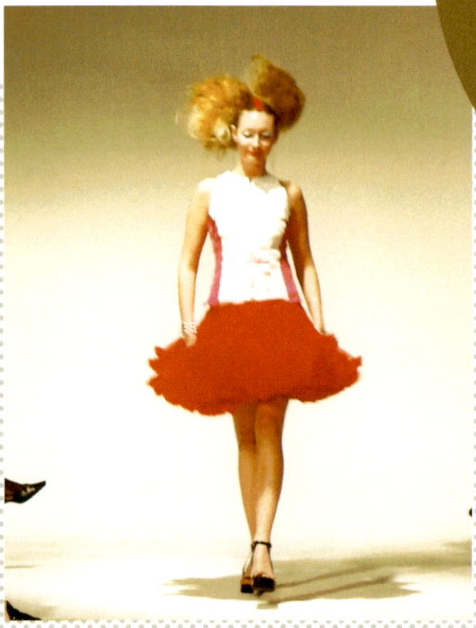

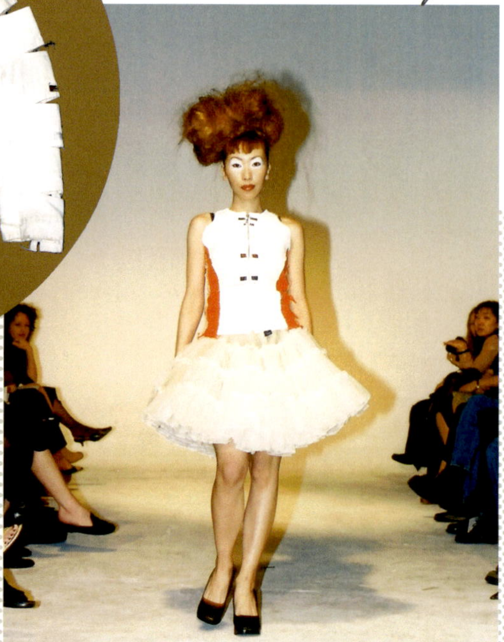

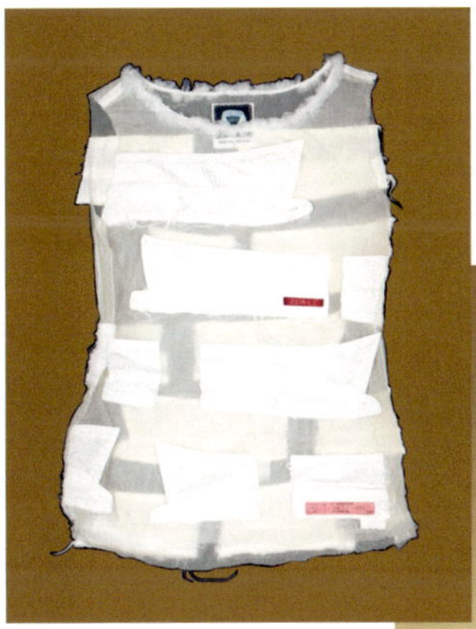

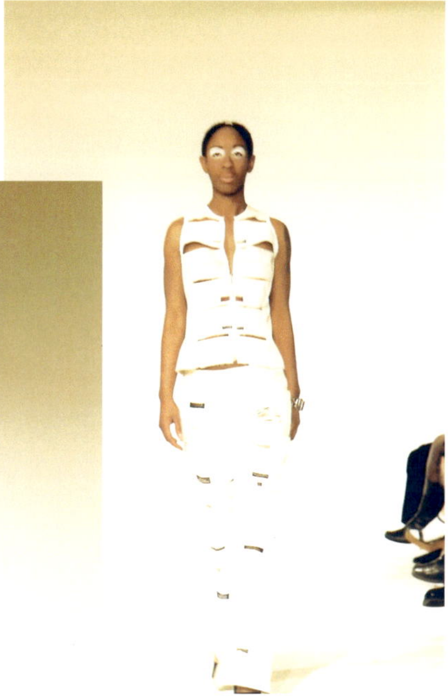

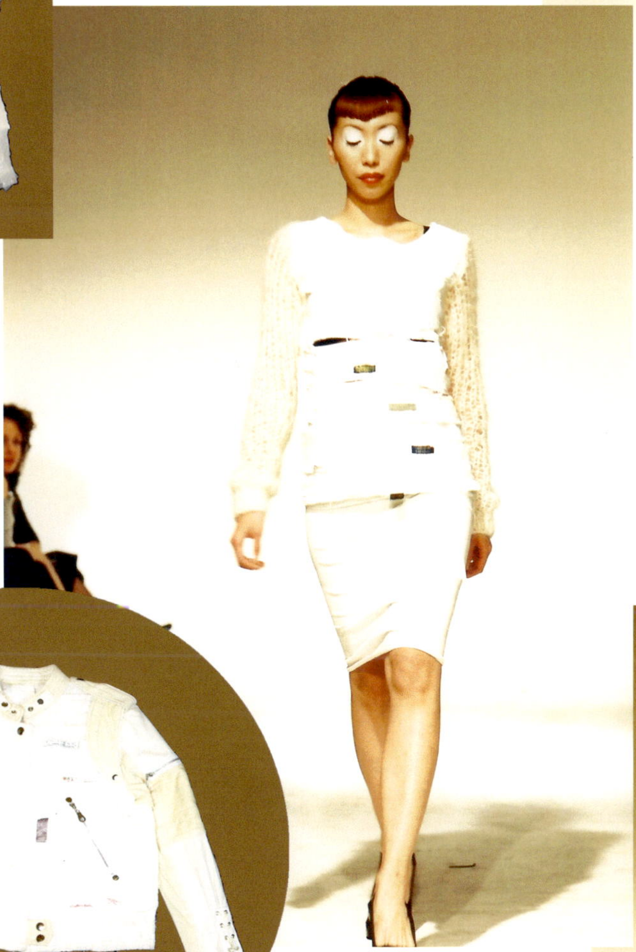

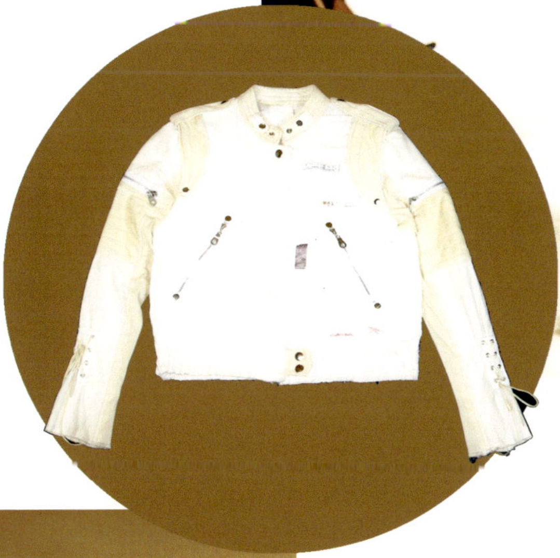

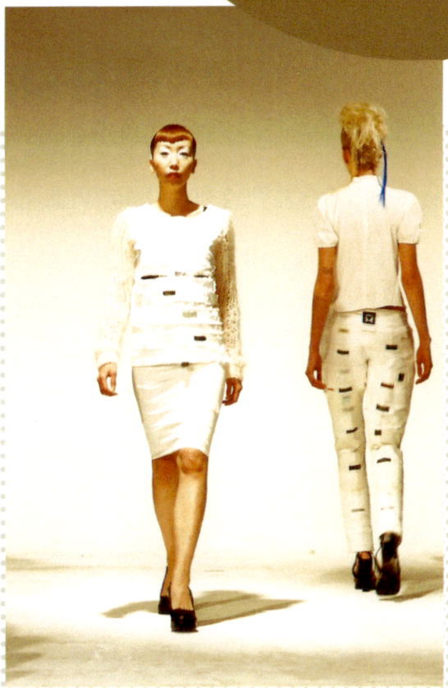

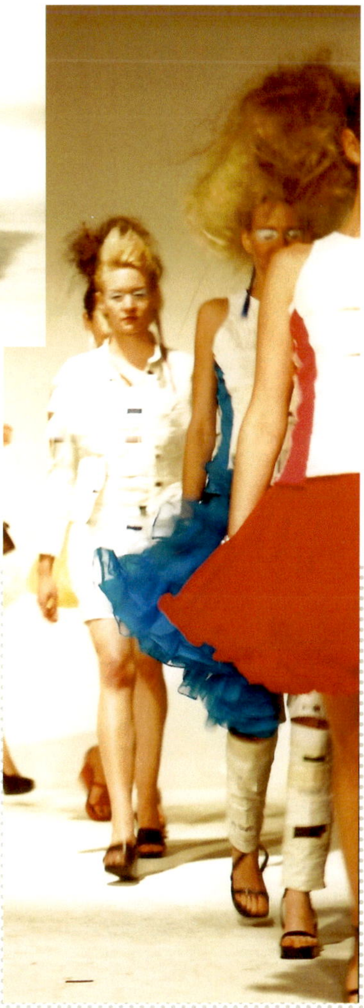

fashion show 2006

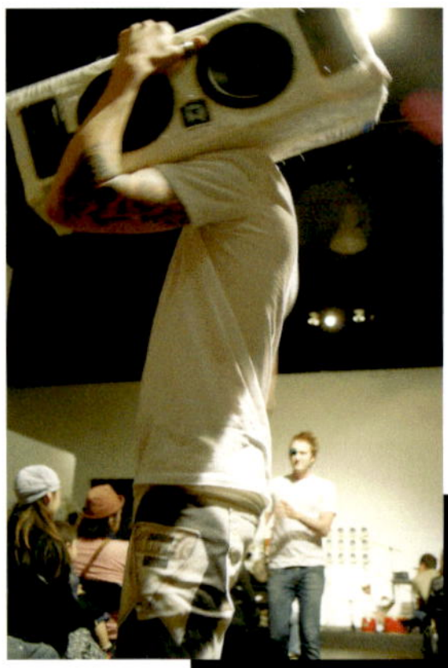

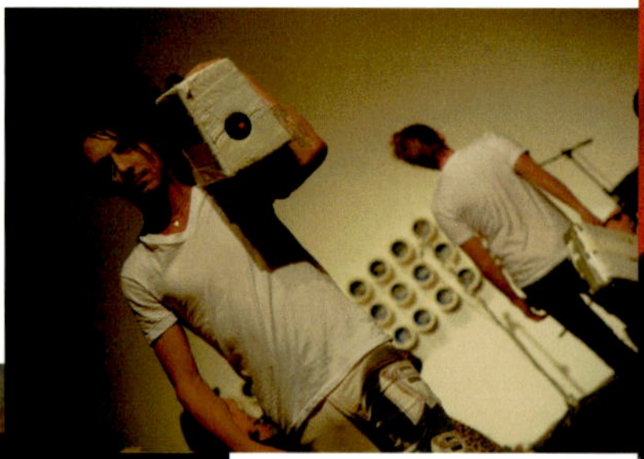

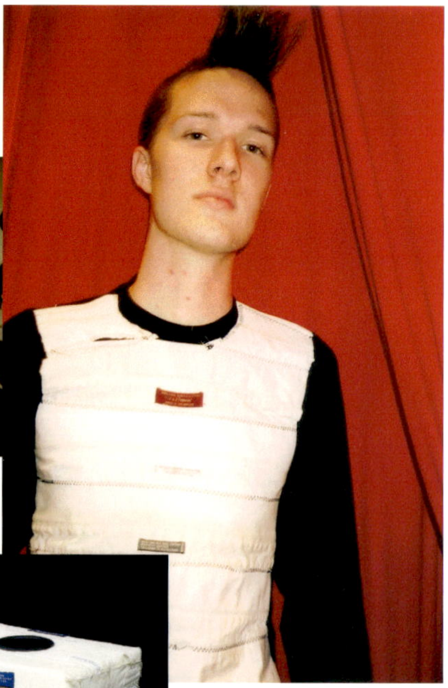

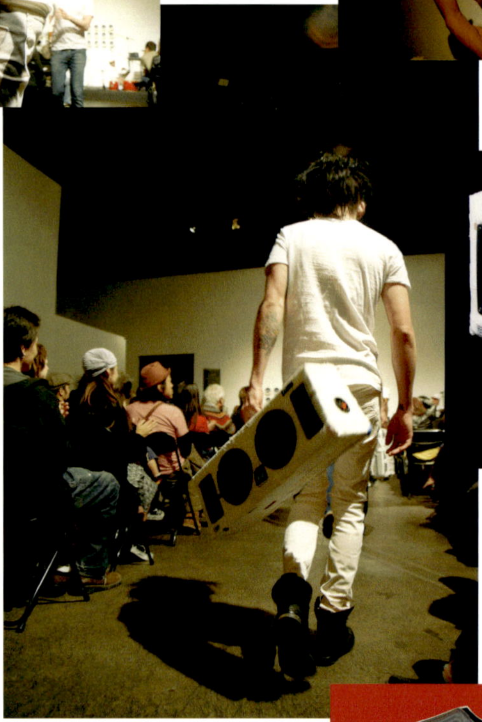

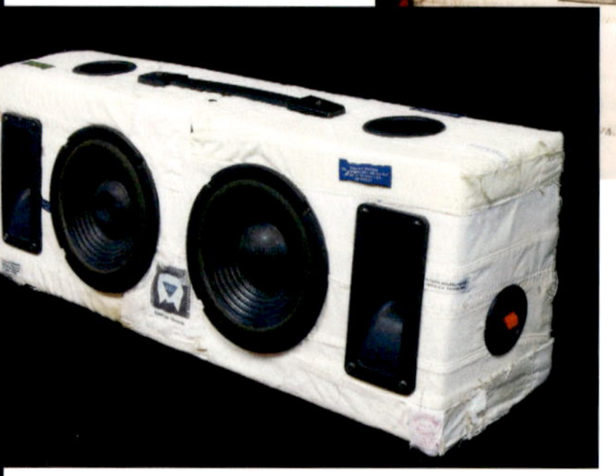

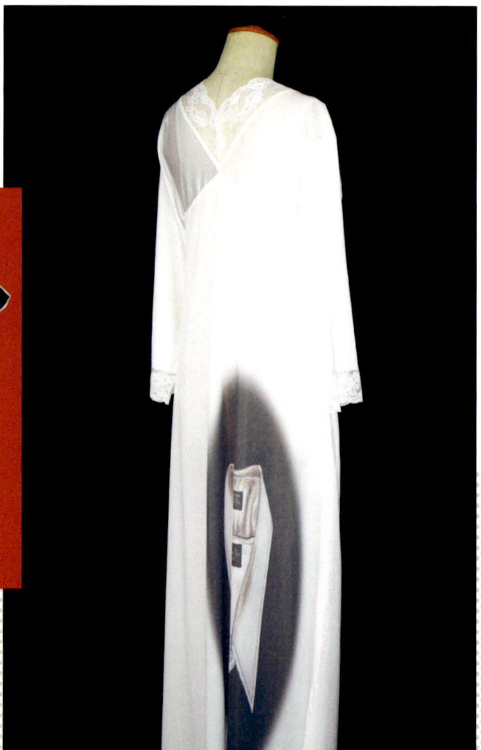

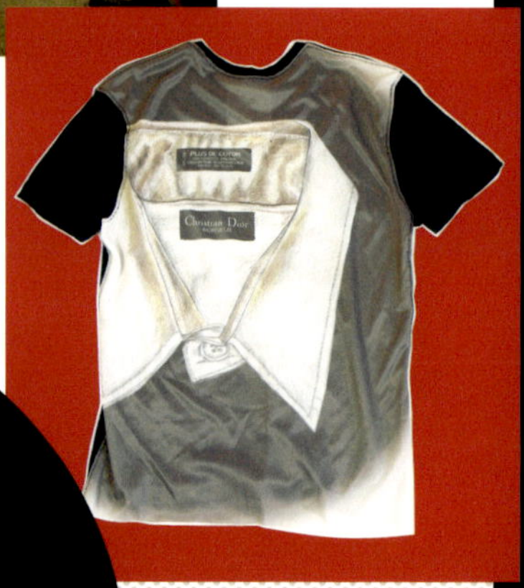

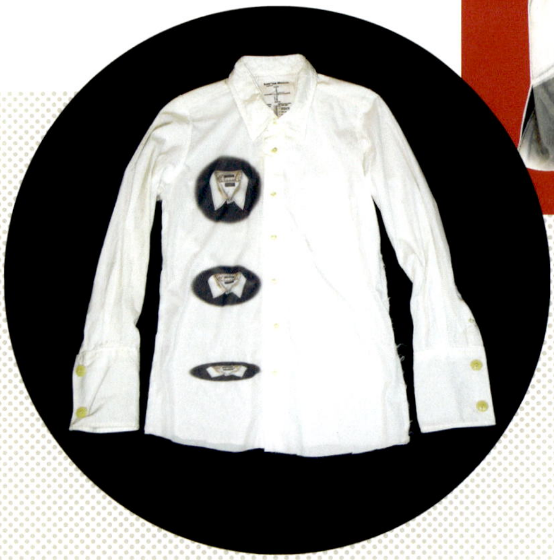

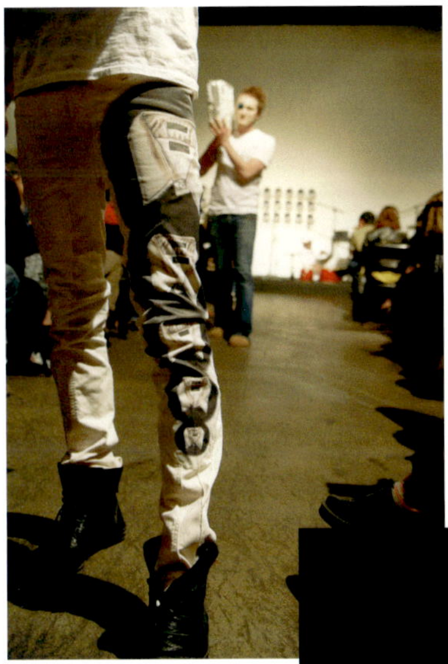
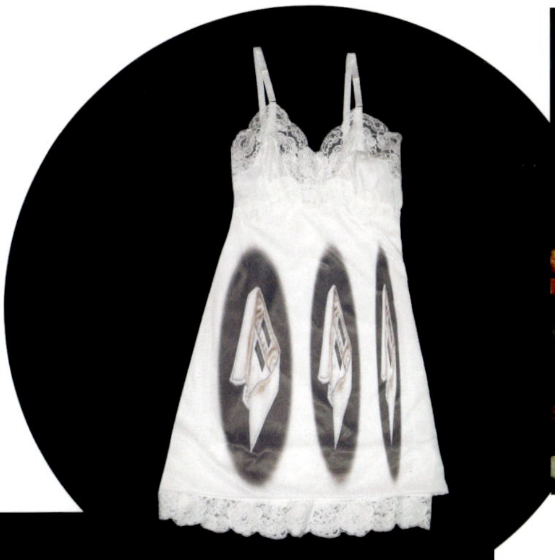
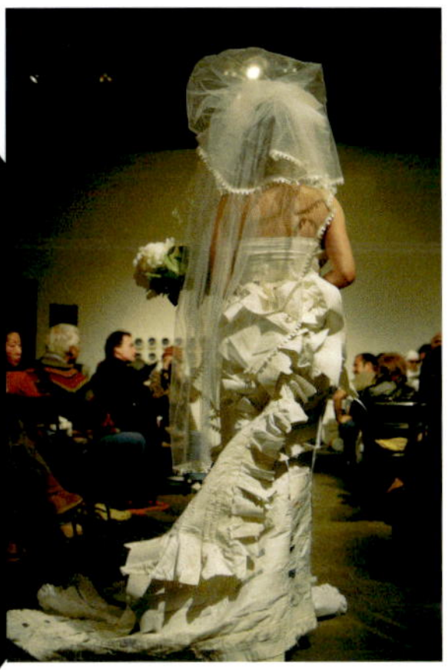
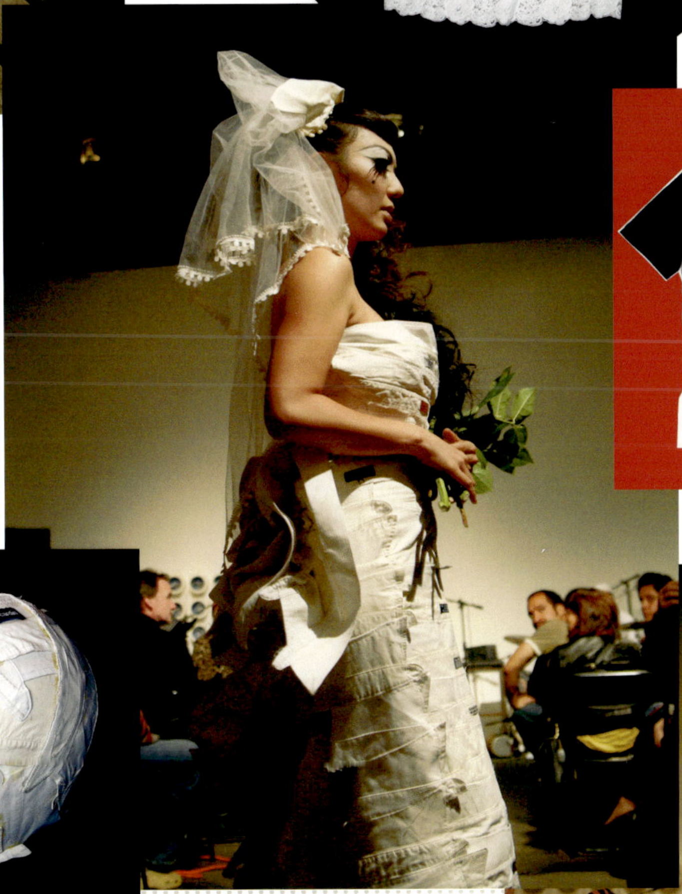
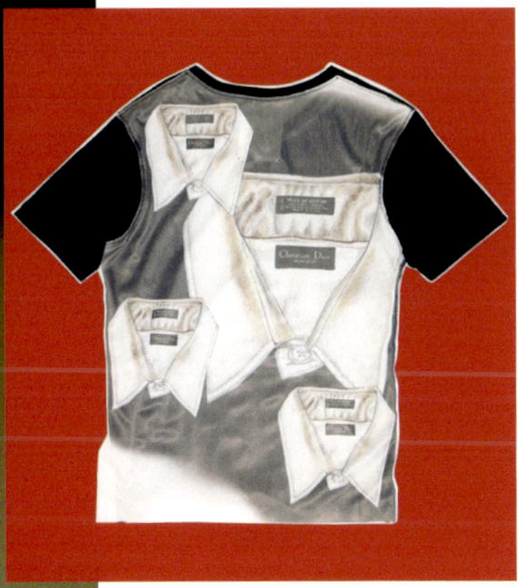
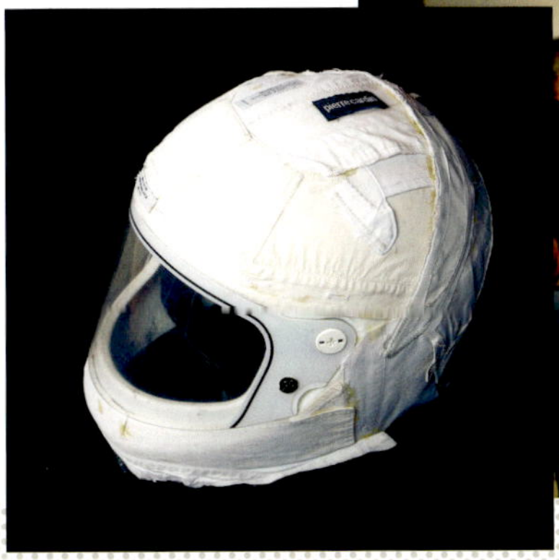
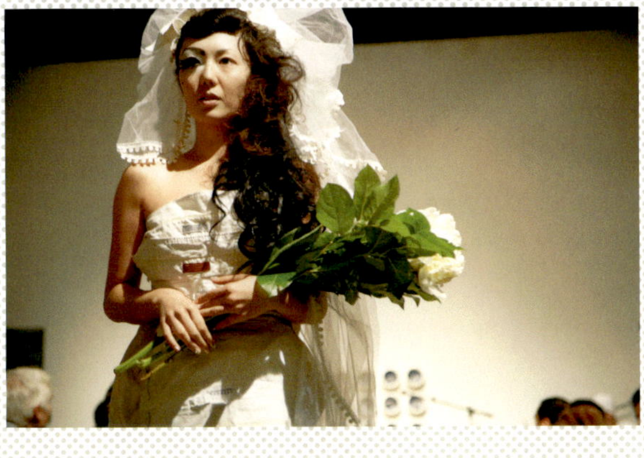
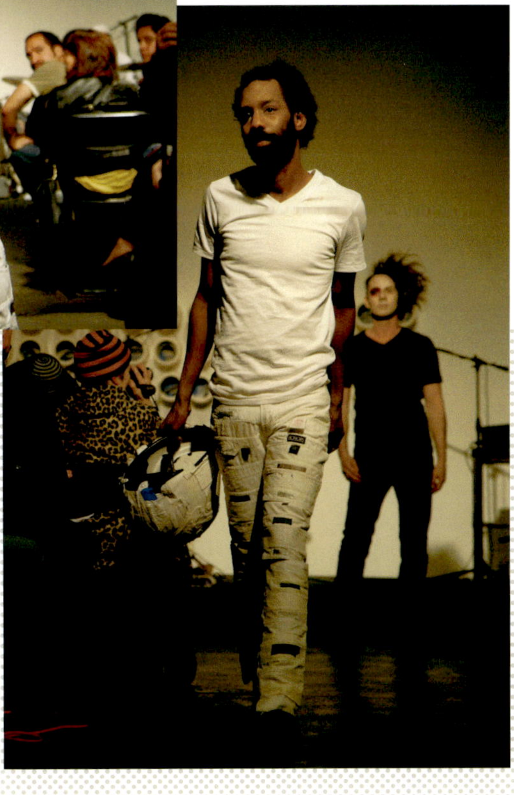

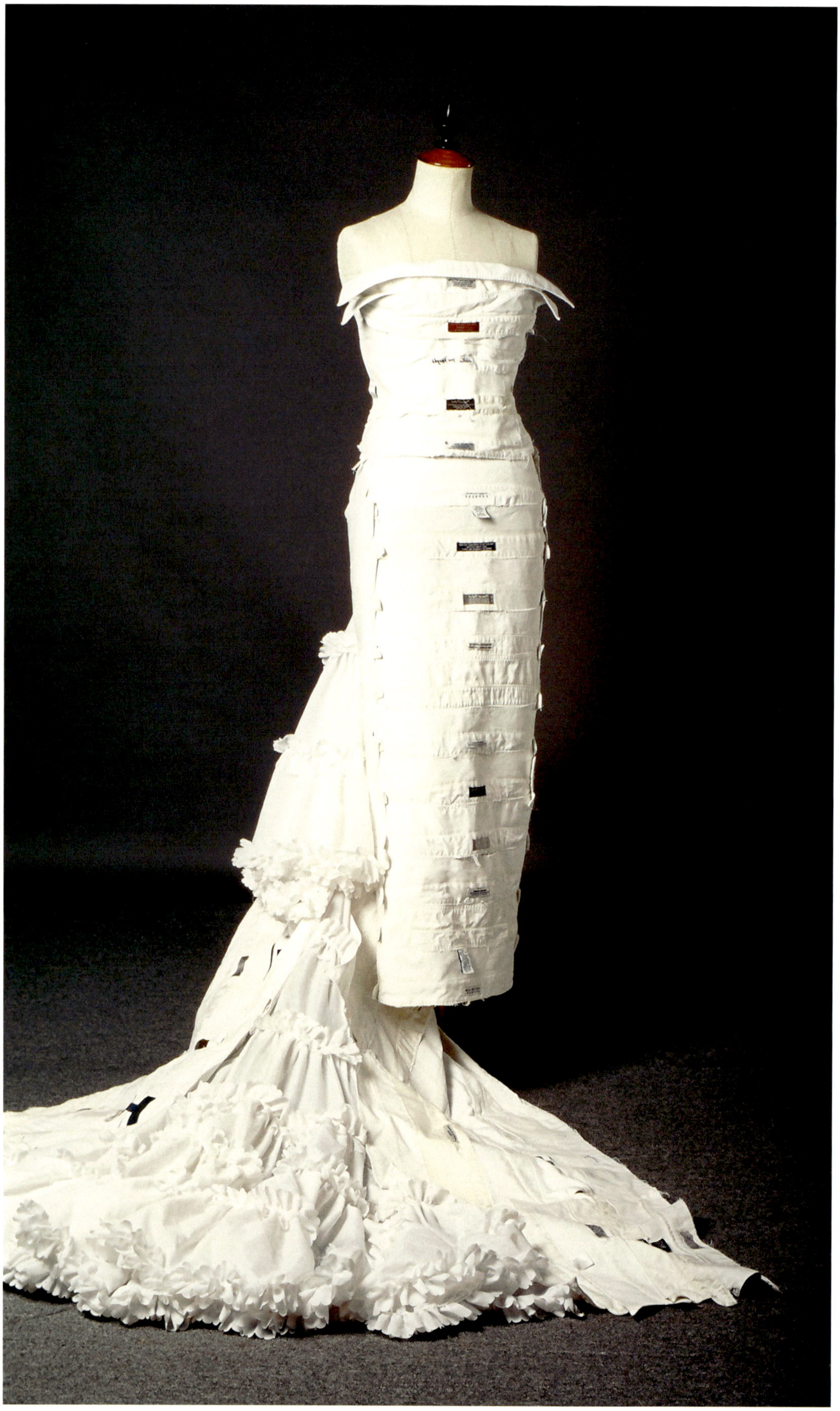

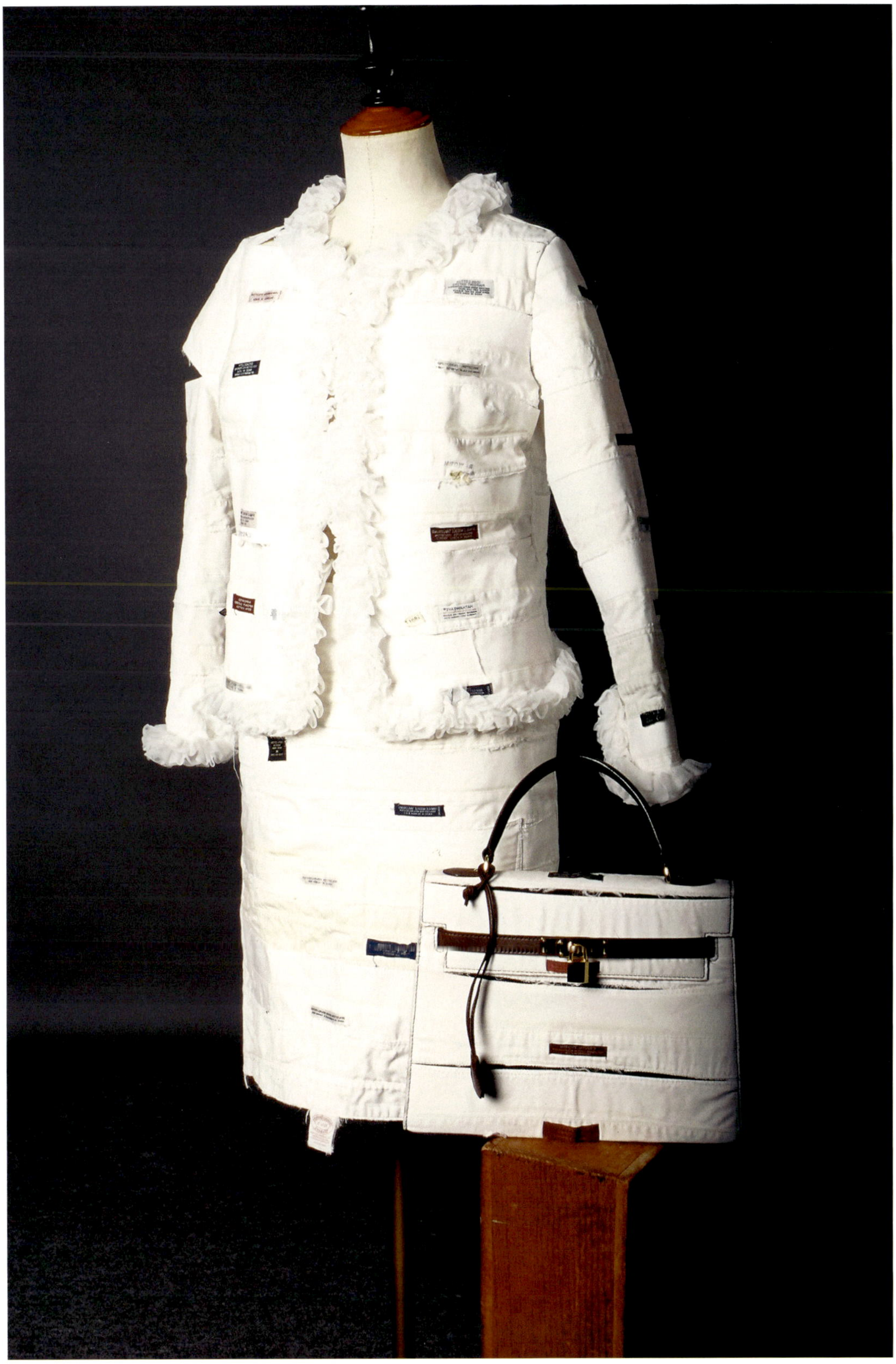

"Collar Noise"

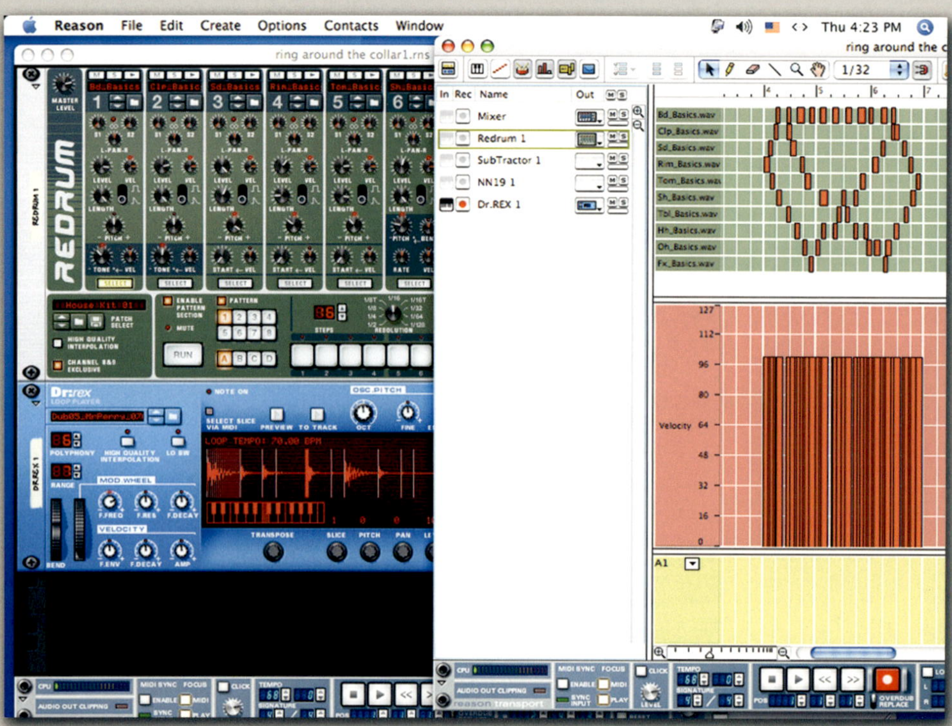

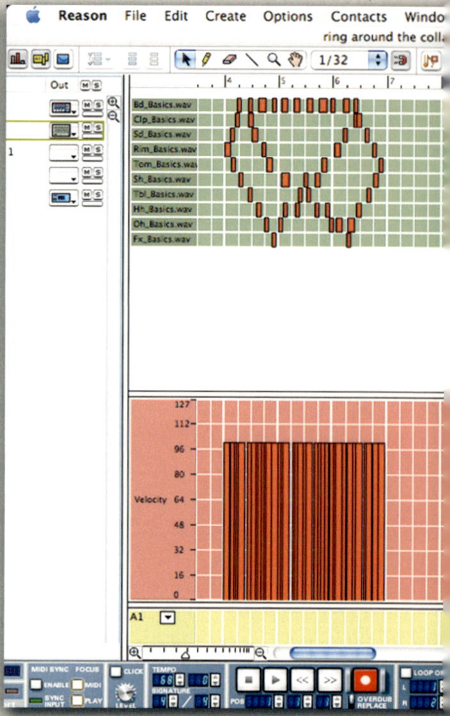

"A Ring Around The Collar Theme" by Les Sewing Sisters

Lyrics by Lun*na Menoh Music by Tsugumi Takashi

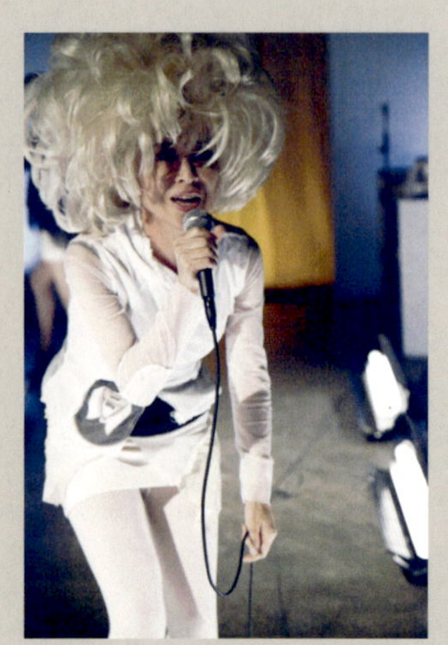

your shirt makes you smart are you satisfied?
just filing a gap: you and how you look

in the closet there is always no hope
i could ask Mr. Machiavelli
how many times he wished he could have more clothes...

my jacket makes my joke ah justified, i am glad
it's never be the same: i and how i look

in the closet there is always too dark
i could ask Mr. Machiavelli
how many times has he changed his clothes and cried?

have you ever seen the collar on your shirt?
the secret stains and tears like a sunset in the sky

have you ever seen what's going on your shirt ?
my arms around your neck and prove all my love

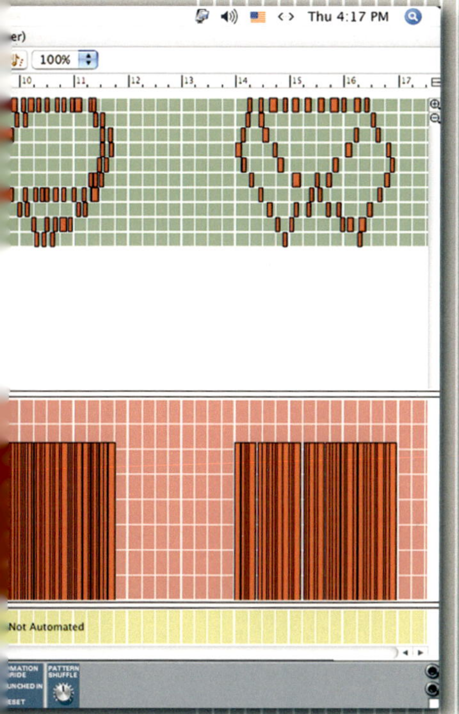
Thu 4:17 PM
100%
Not Automated

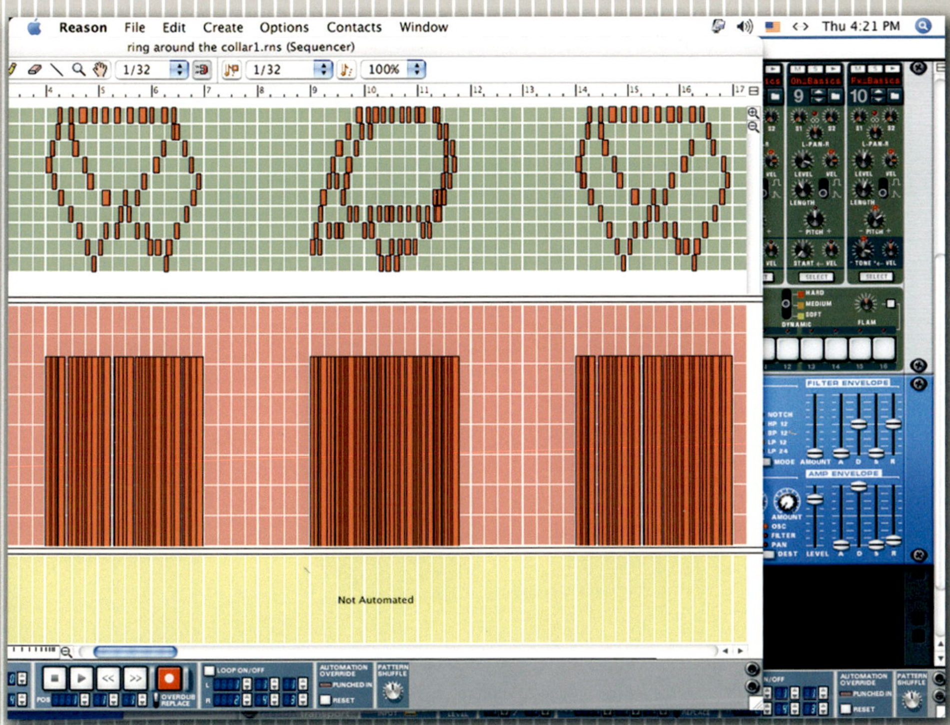
Reason File Edit Create Options Contacts Window
ring around the collar1.rns (Sequencer)
Thu 4:21 PM
1/32
1/32
100%
Not Automated
FILTER ENVELOPE
AMP ENVELOPE
AUTOMATION OVERRIDE
PATTERN SHUFFLE

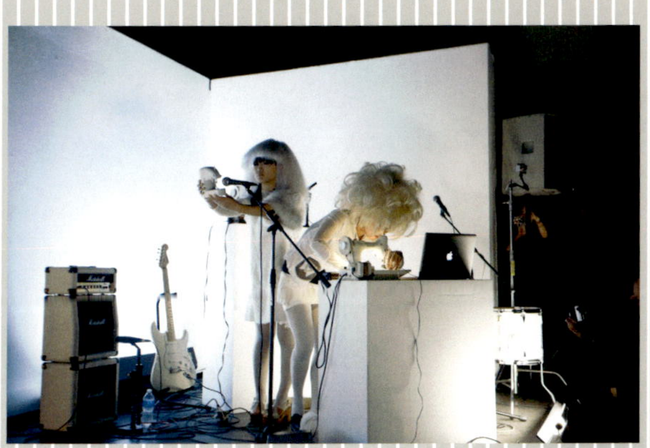

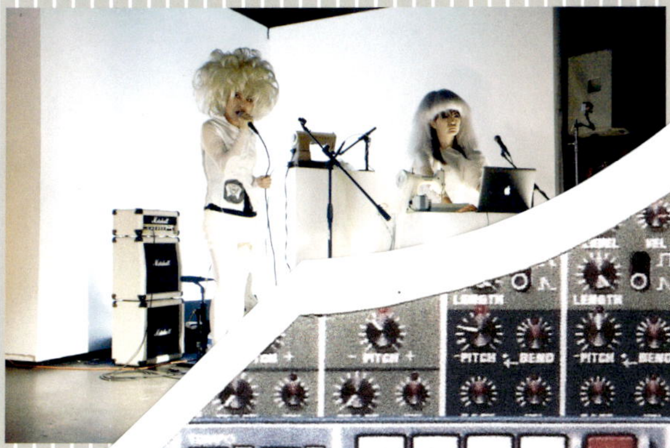

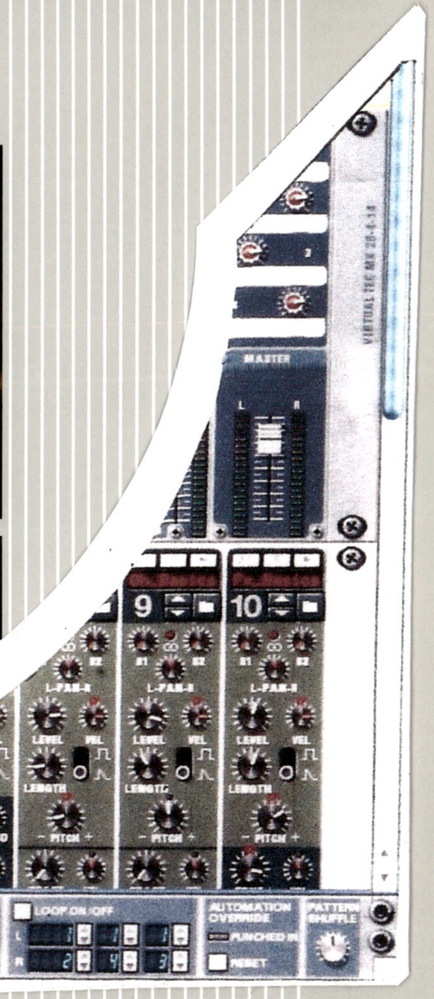
MASTER
LOOP ON/OFF
AUTOMATION OVERRIDE
PUNCHED IN
RESET
PATTERN SHUFFLE

Dirty Collar Paintings

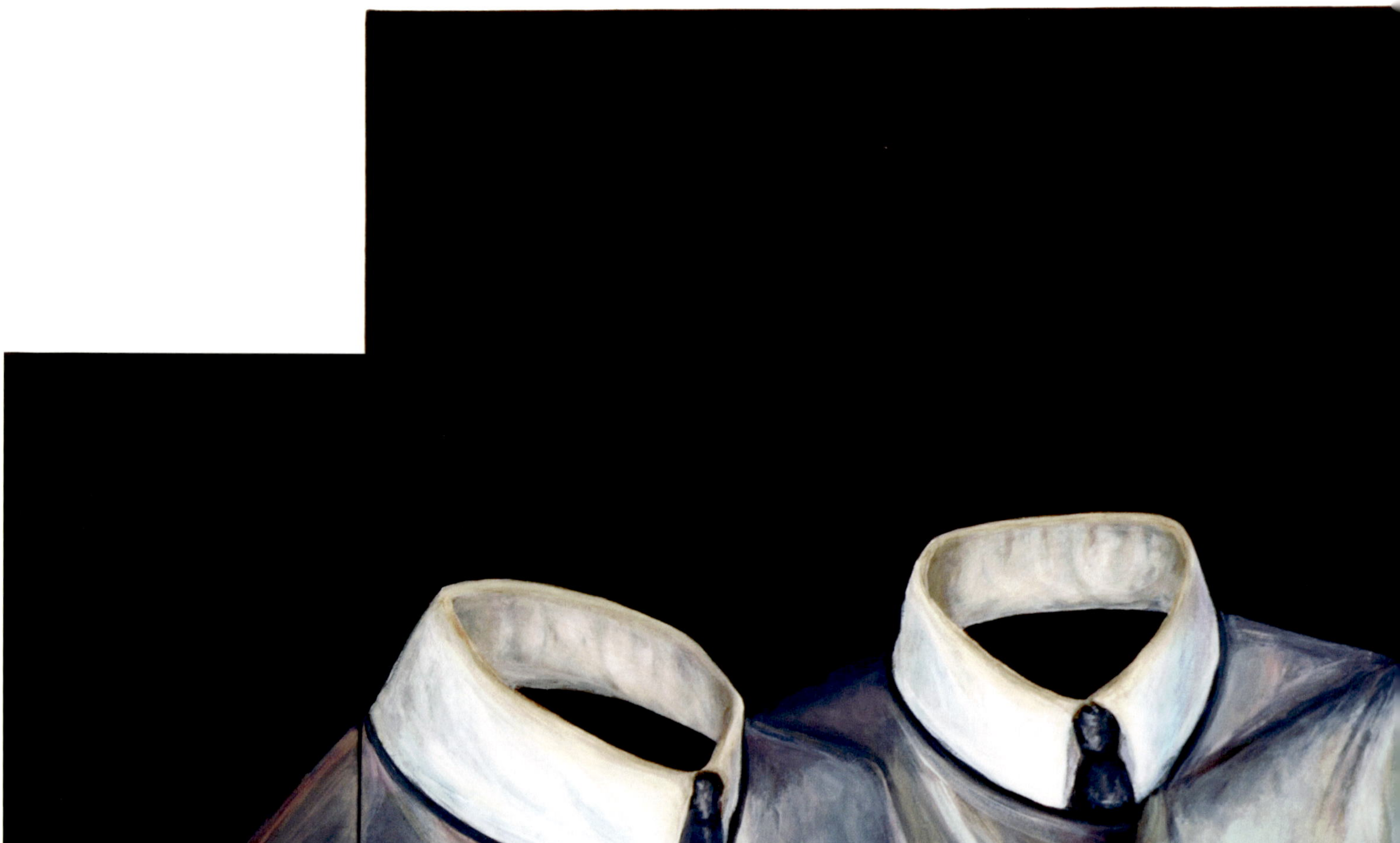

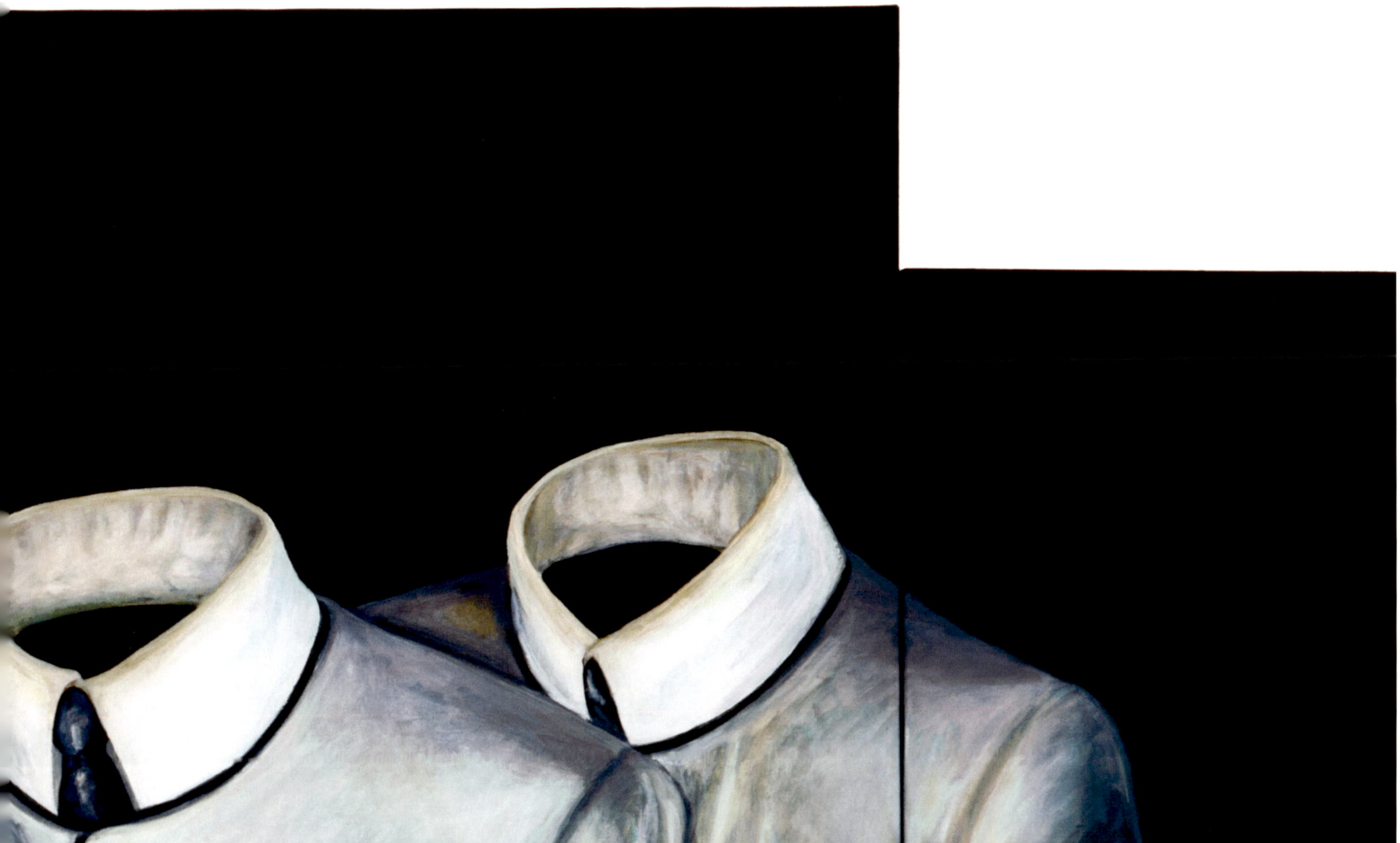

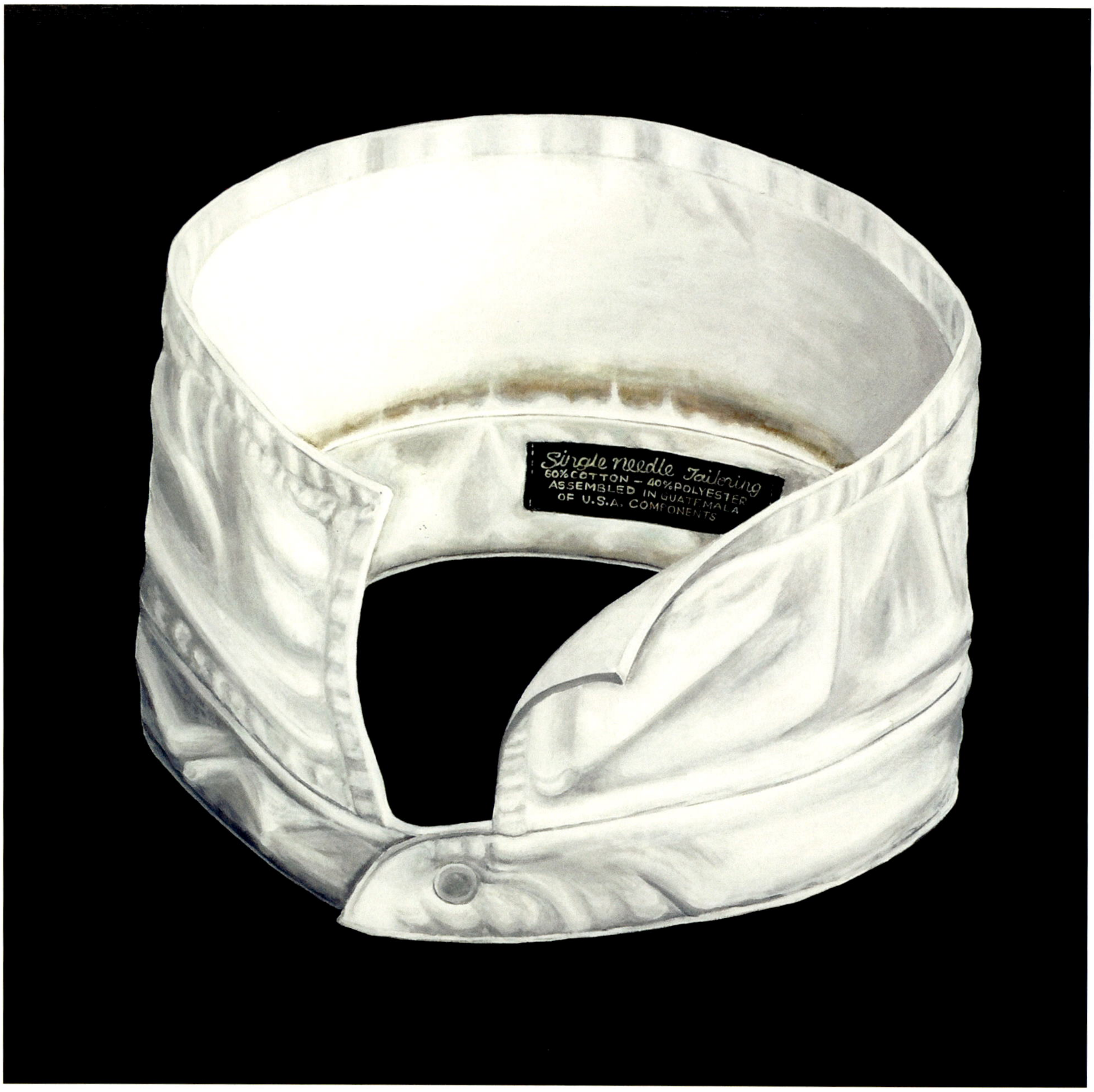
Single needle Tailoring
60% COTTON – 40% POLYESTER
ASSEMBLED IN GUATEMALA
OF U.S.A. COMPONENTS

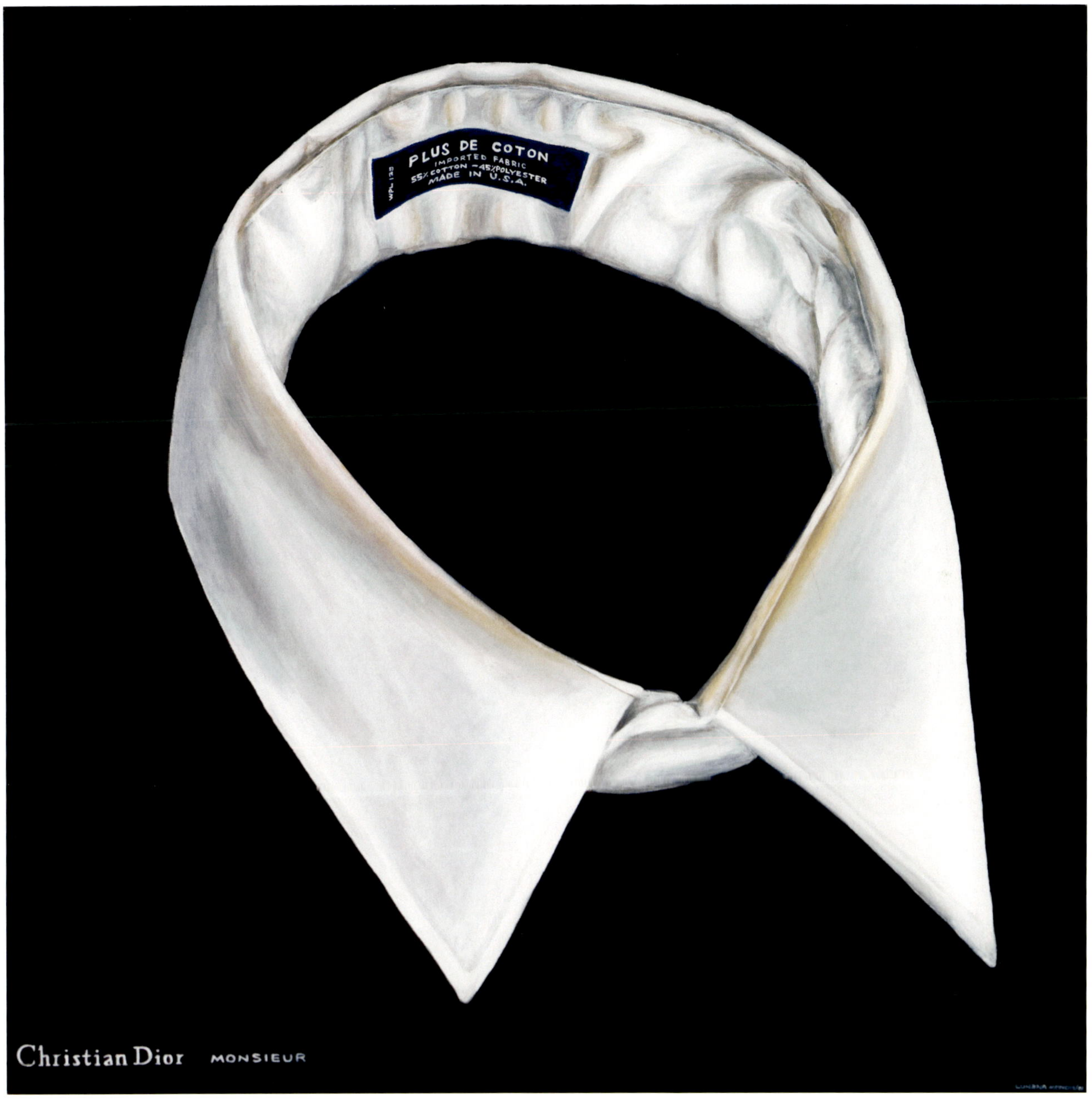
PLUS DE COTON
IMPORTED FABRIC
55% COTTON - 45% POLYESTER
MADE IN U.S.A.
Christian Dior MONSIEUR

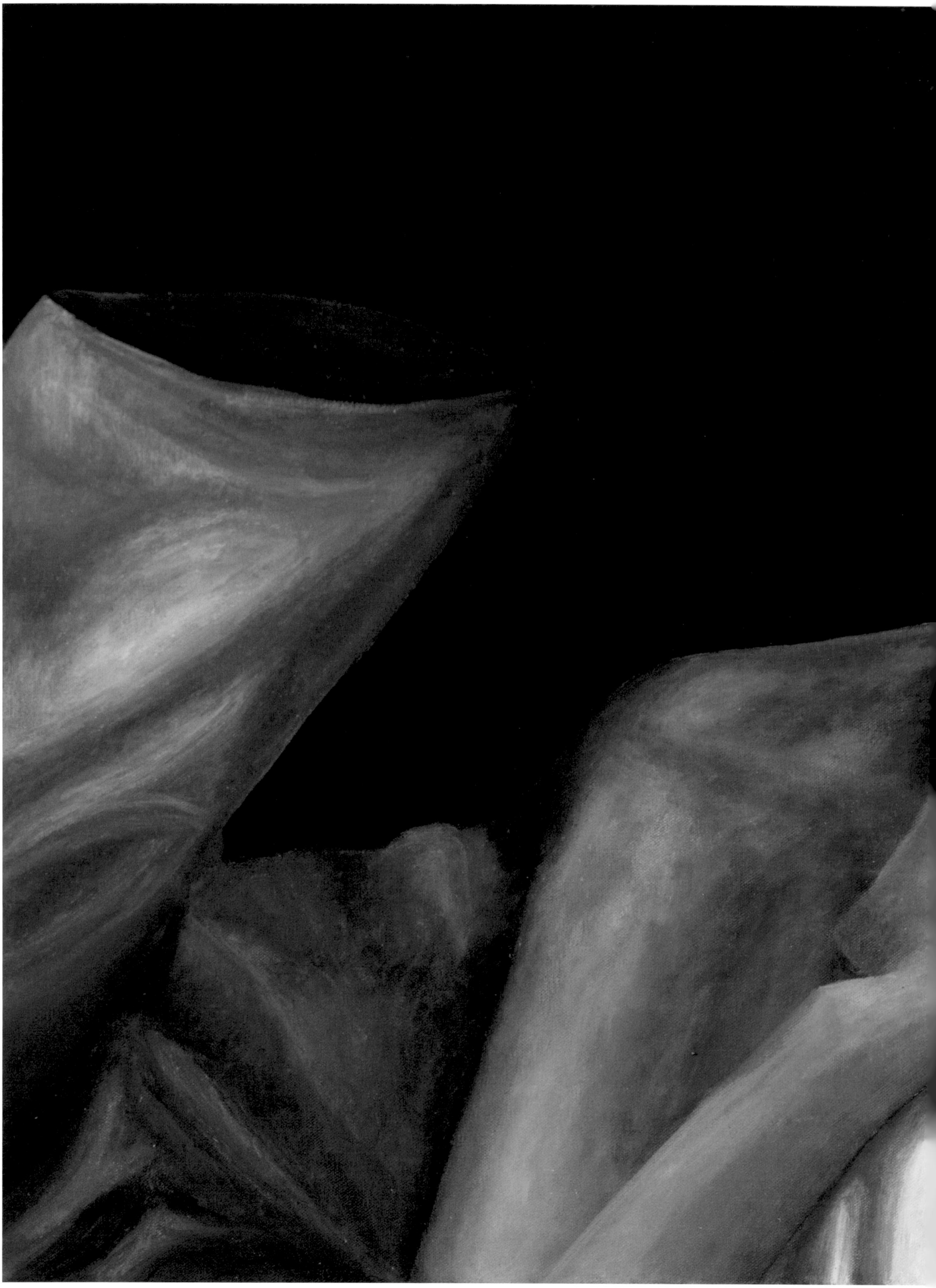

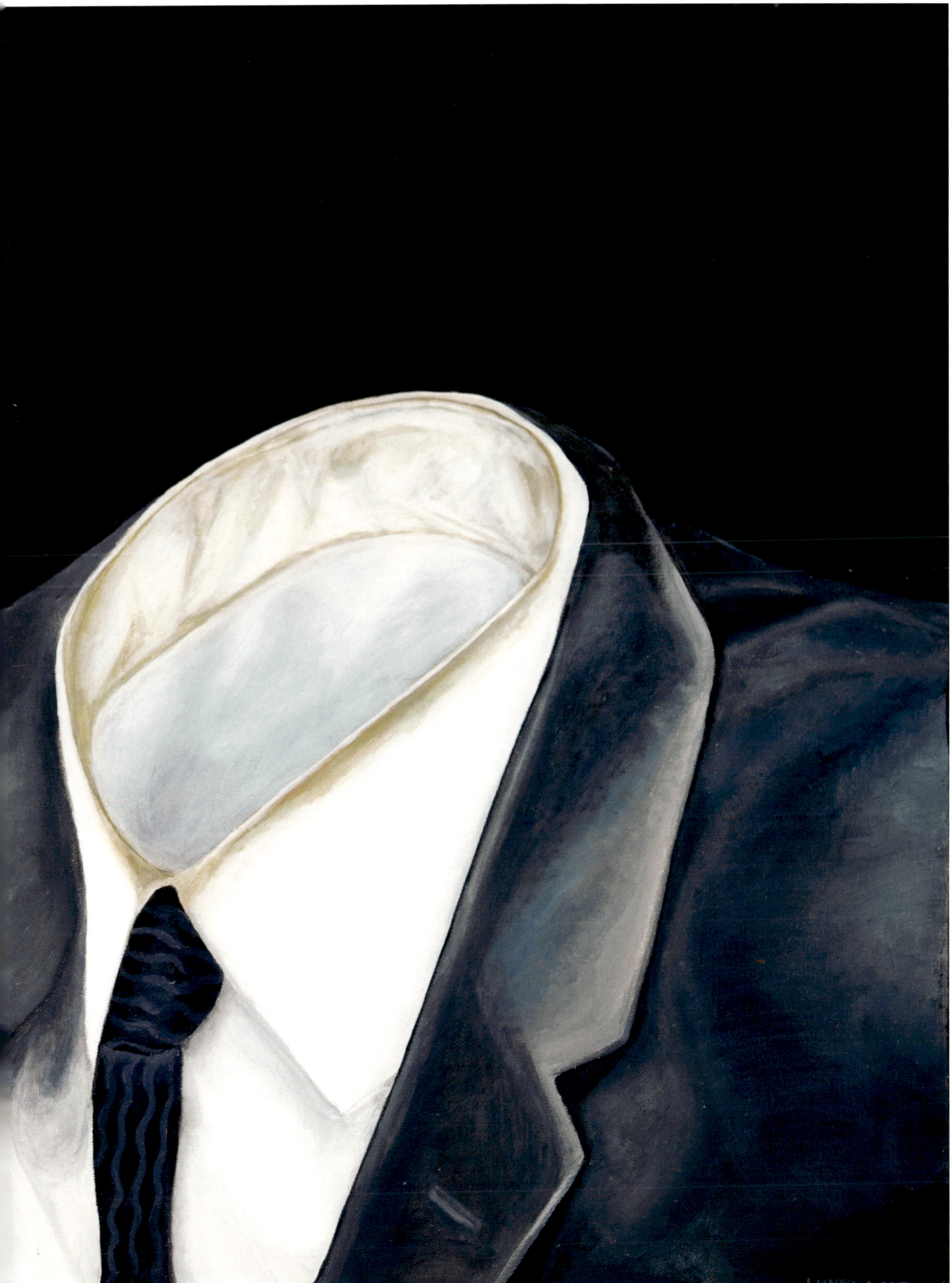
LUN*NA MENON

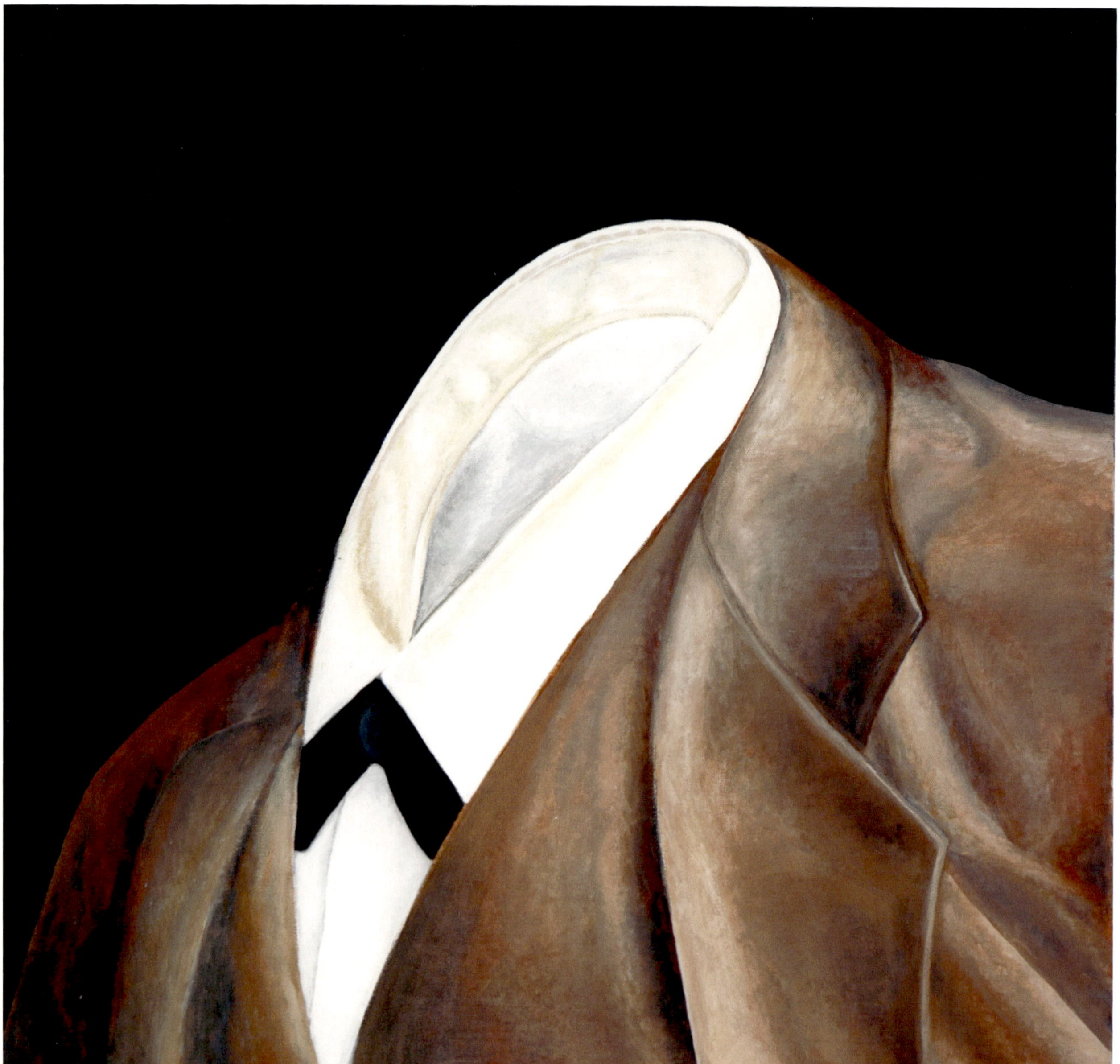

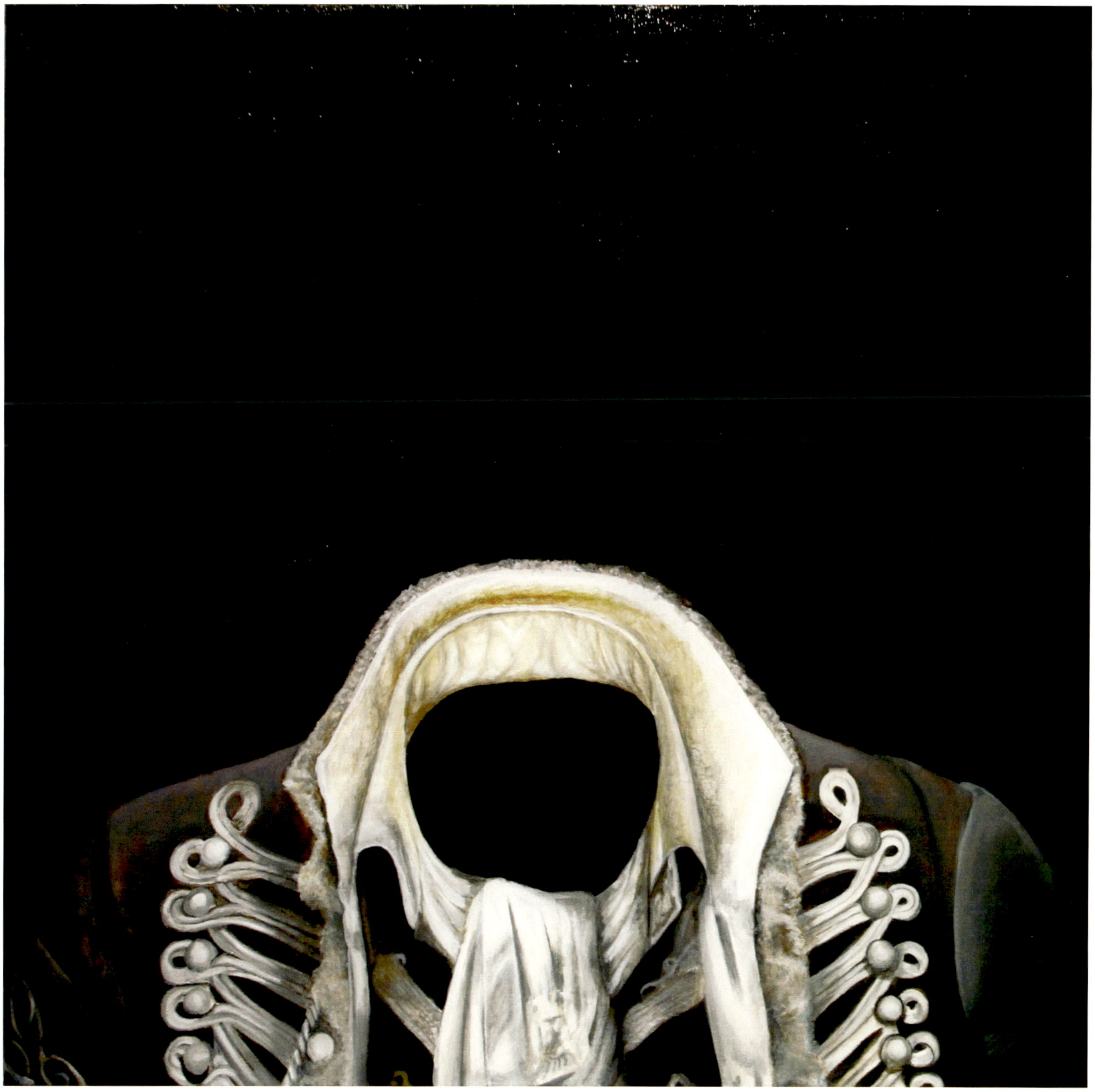

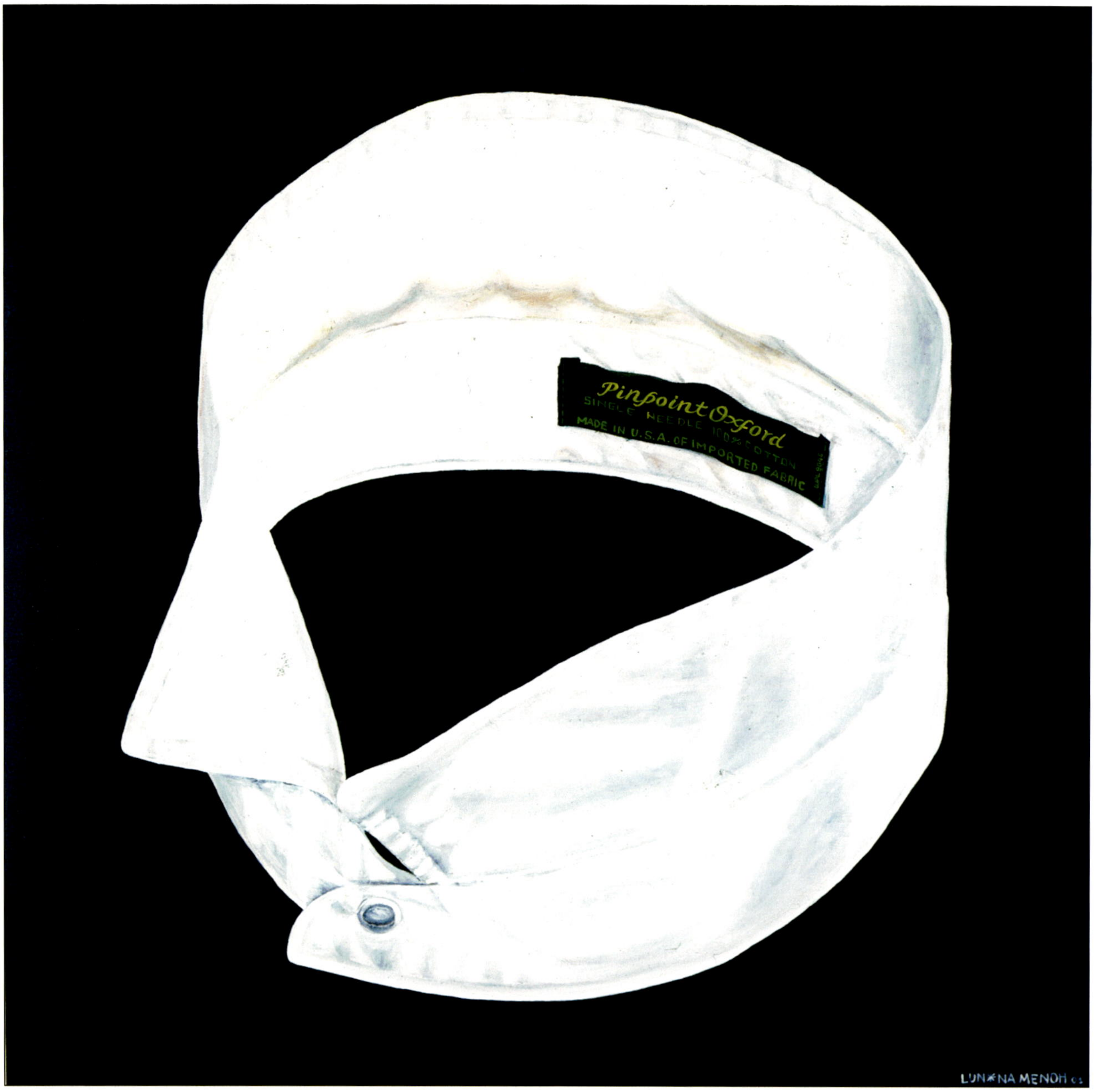
Pinpoint Oxford
SINGLE NEEDLE 100% COTTON
MADE IN U.S.A. OF IMPORTED FABRIC
LUN*NA MENOH

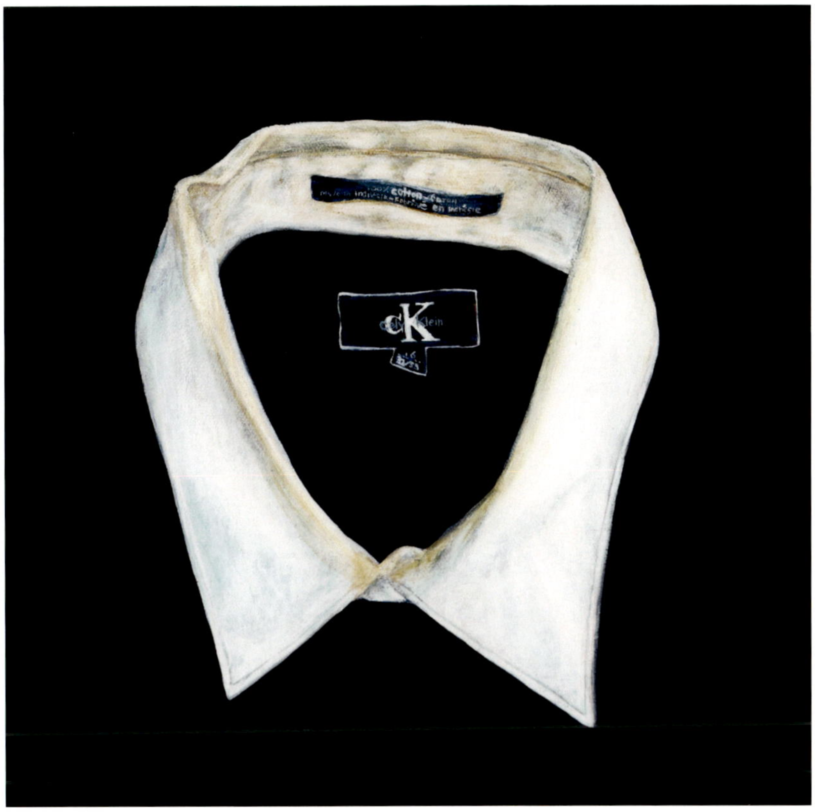

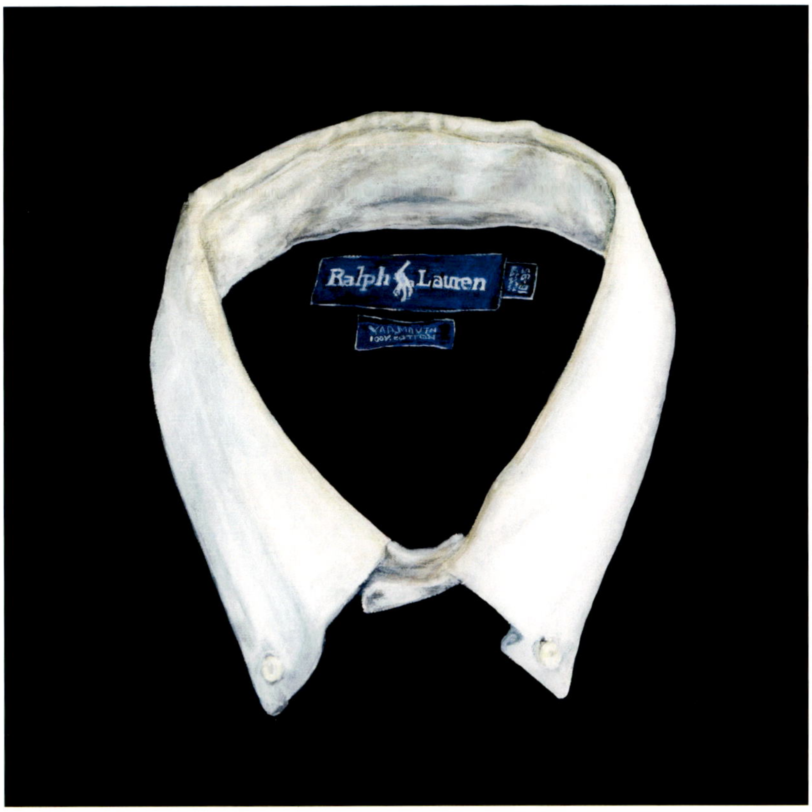
Ralph Lauren

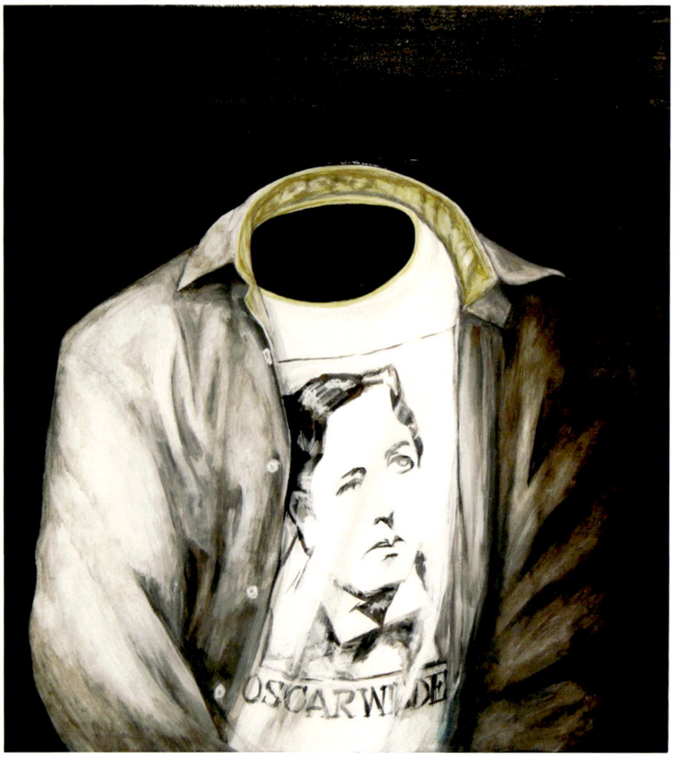
OSCAR WILDE

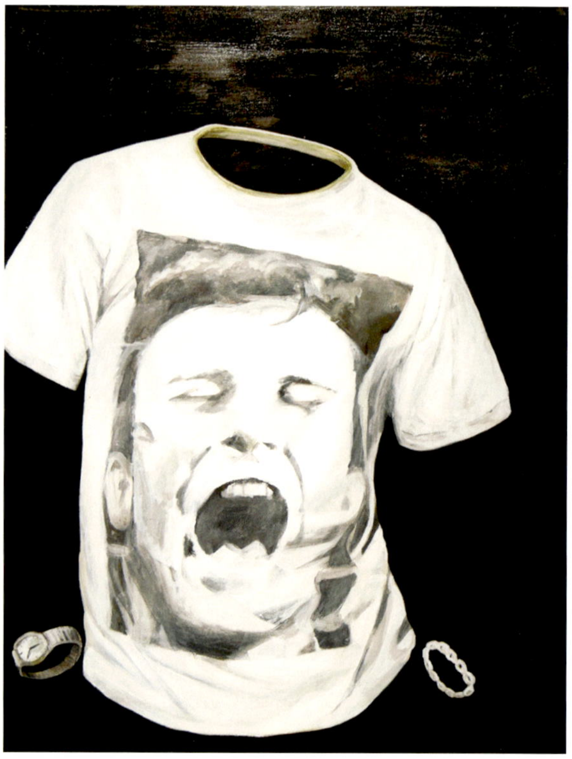

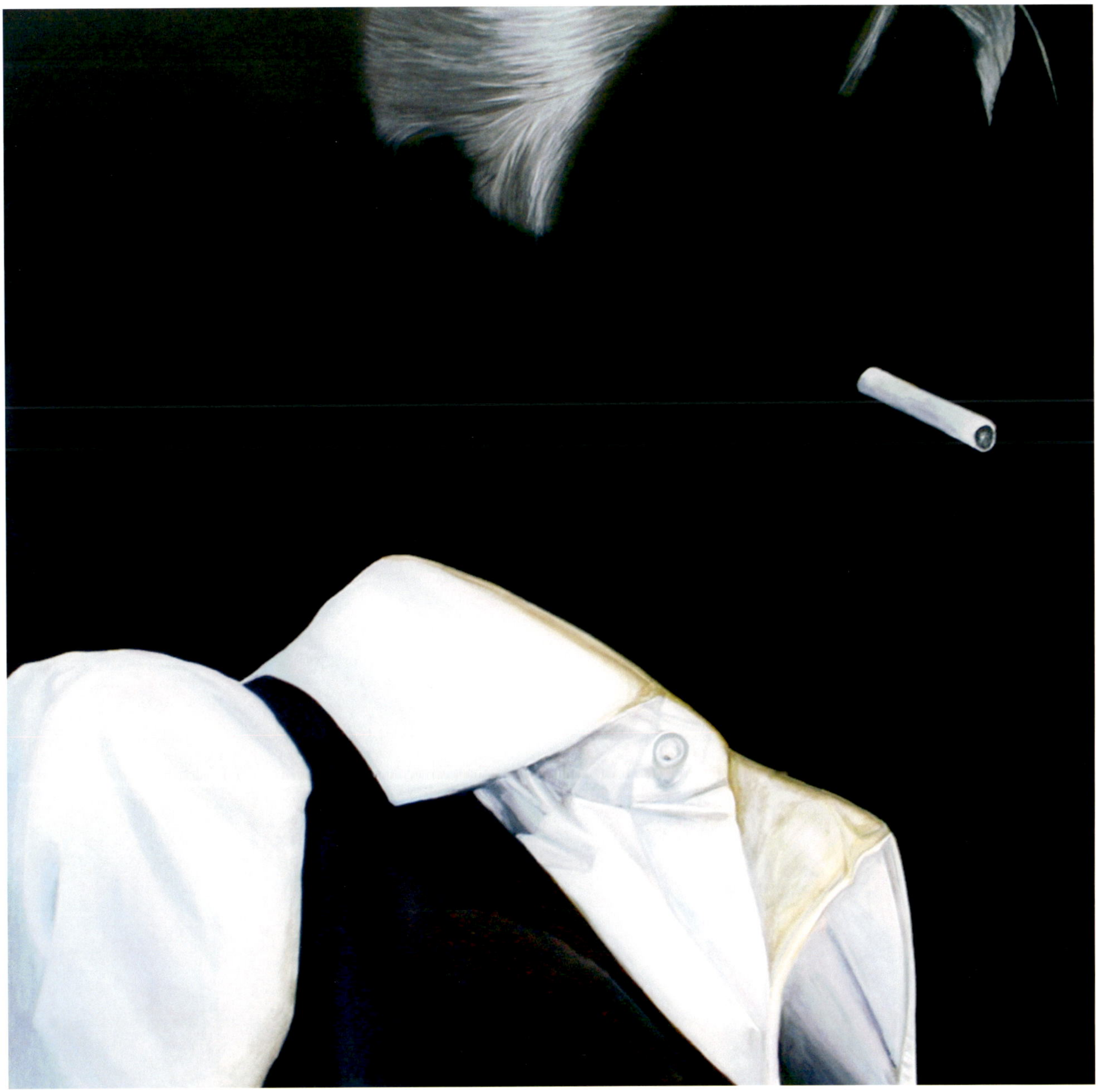

Installation

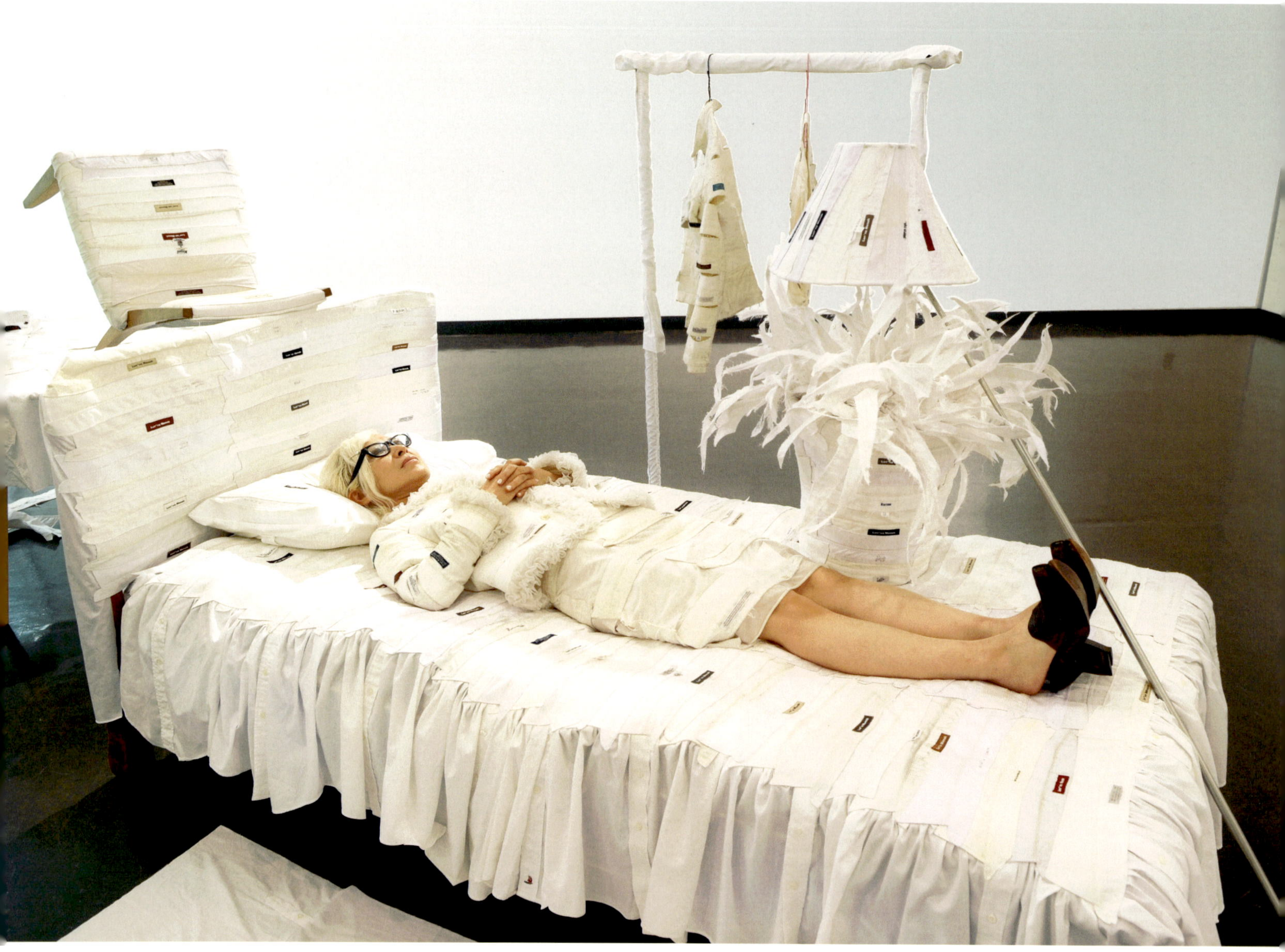

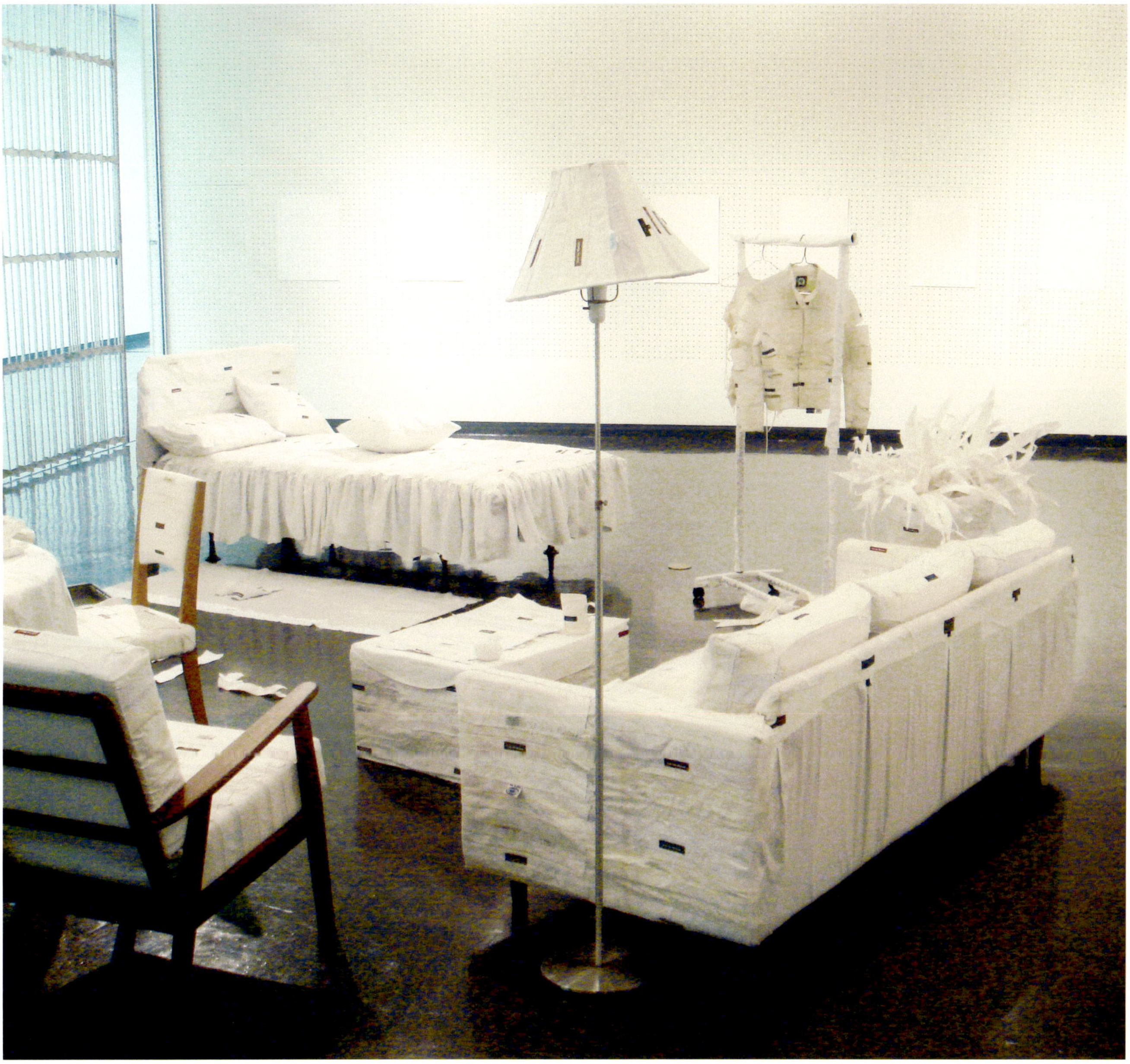

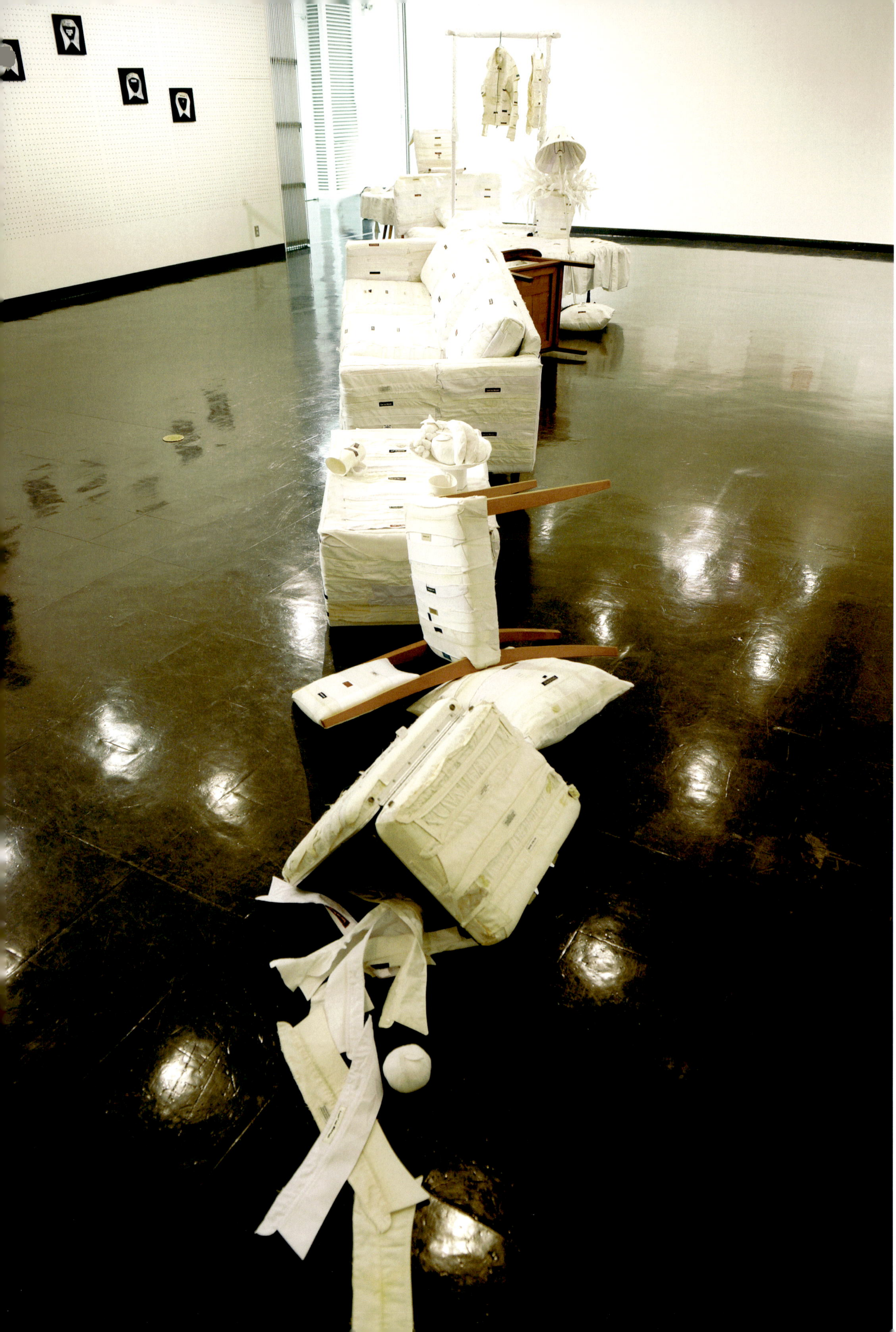

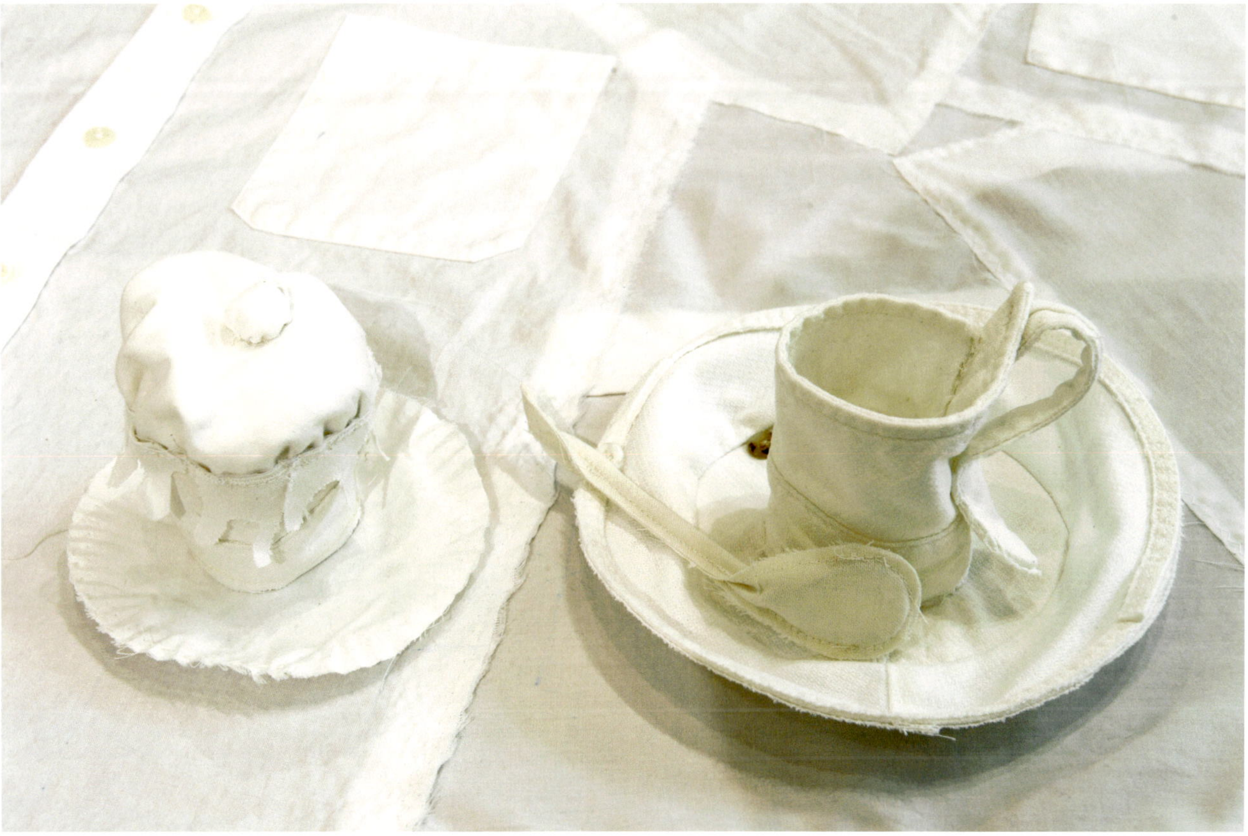

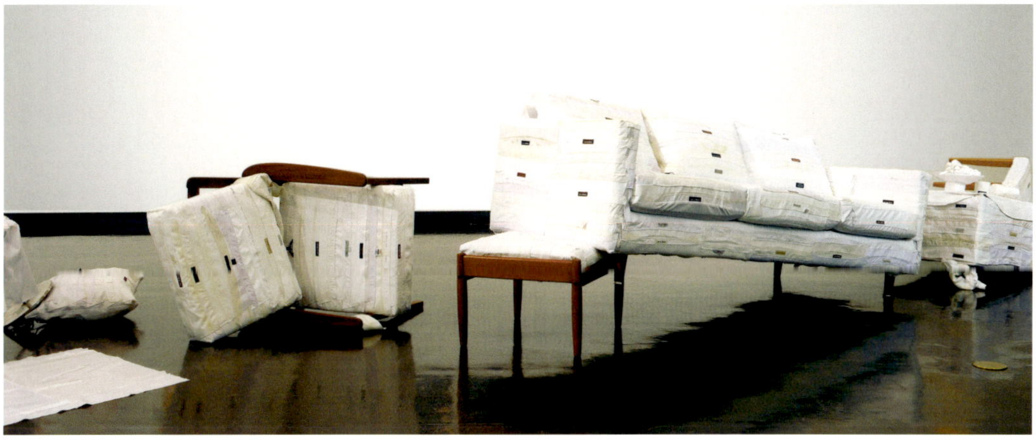

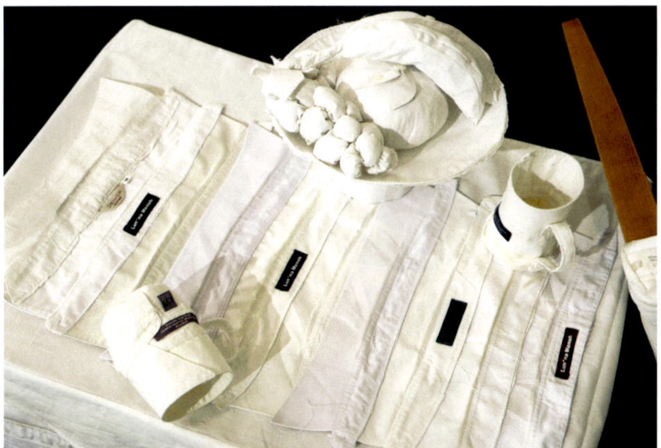

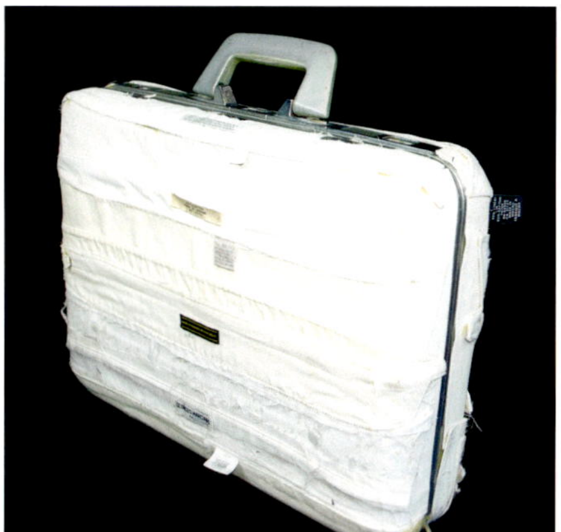

Sculptures

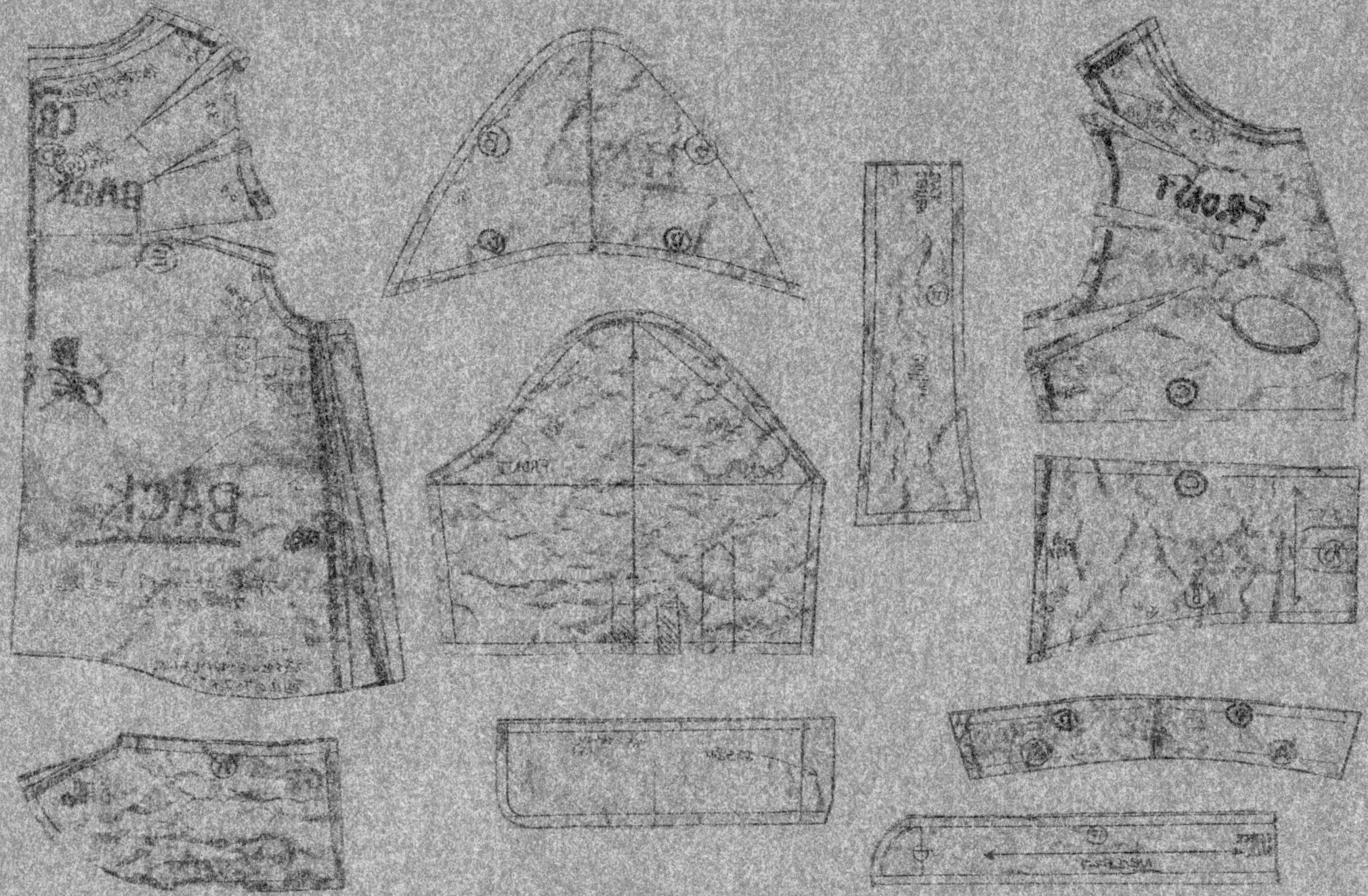
BACK

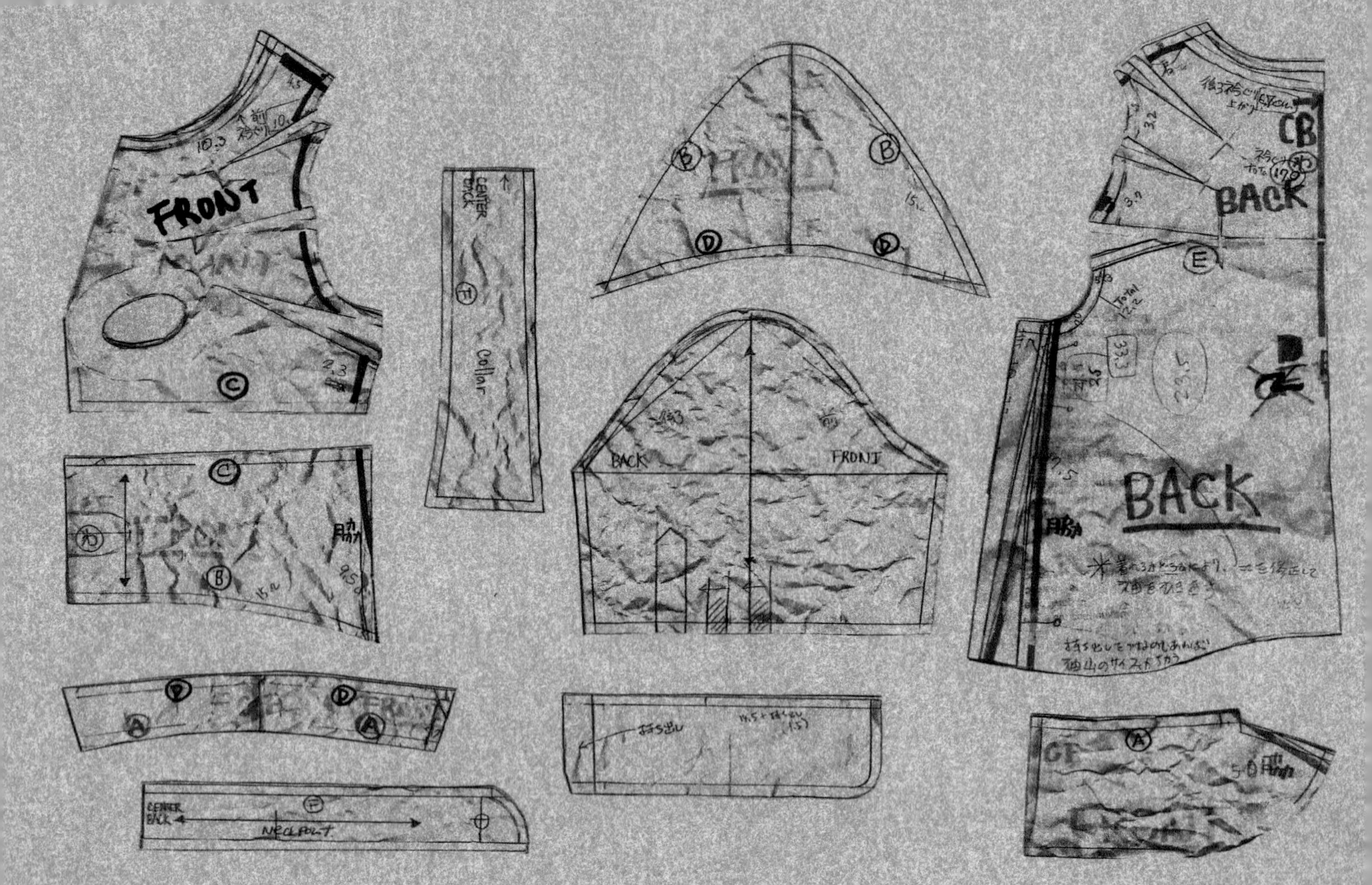
FRONT
CENTER BACK
Collar
BACK
FRONT
CB
BACK
BACK
CENTER BACK
NECKPOINT
CF

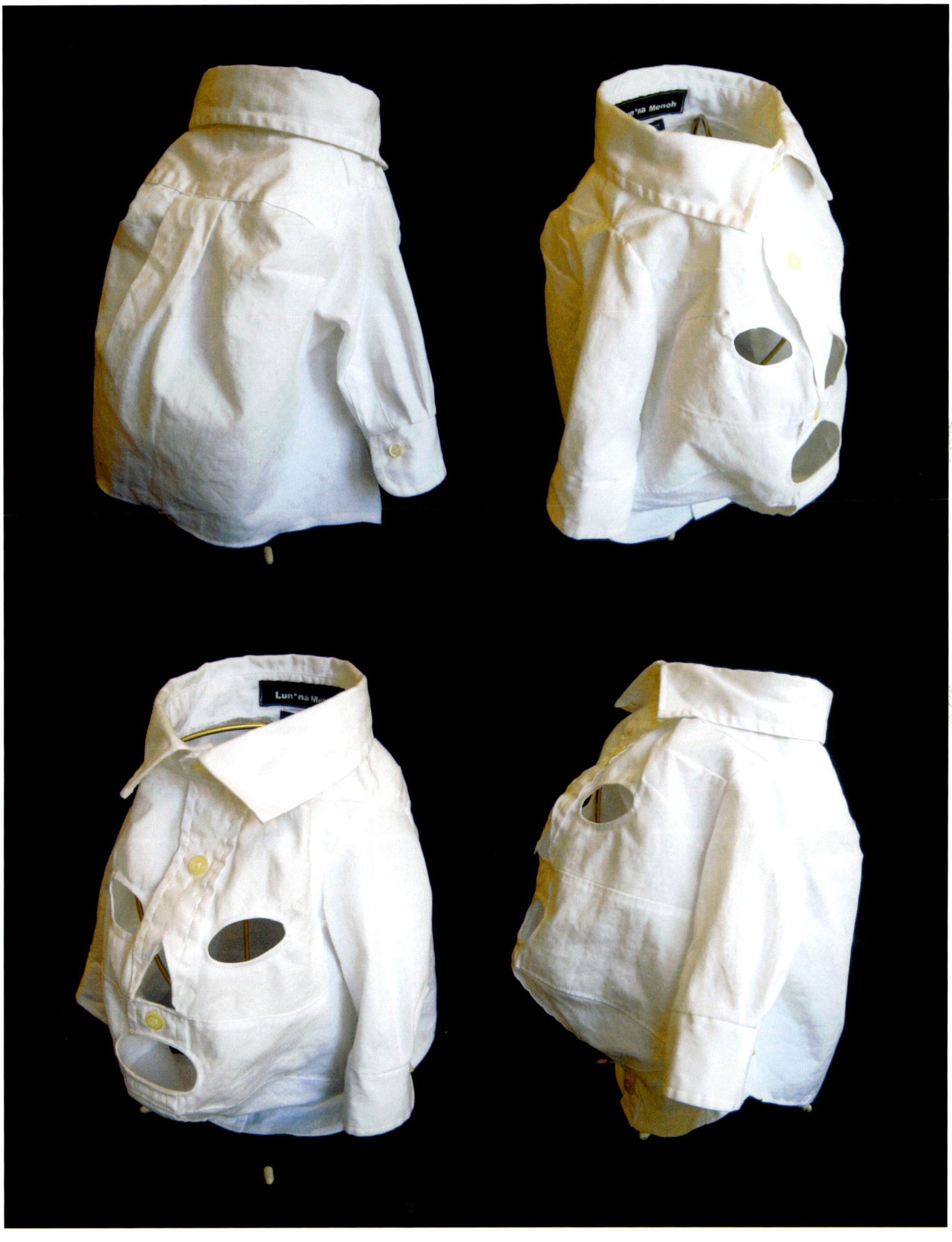

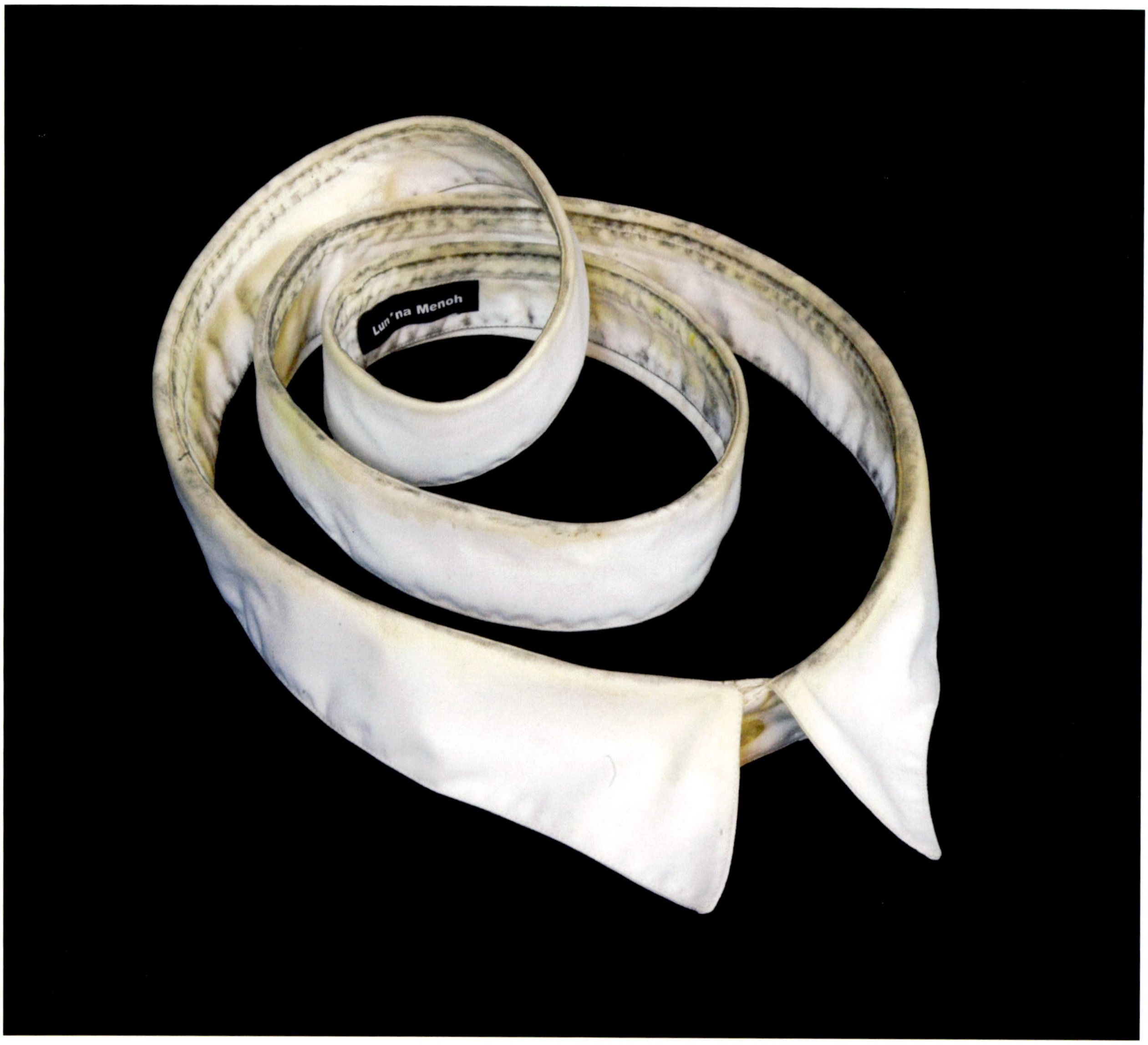
Lun'na Menoh

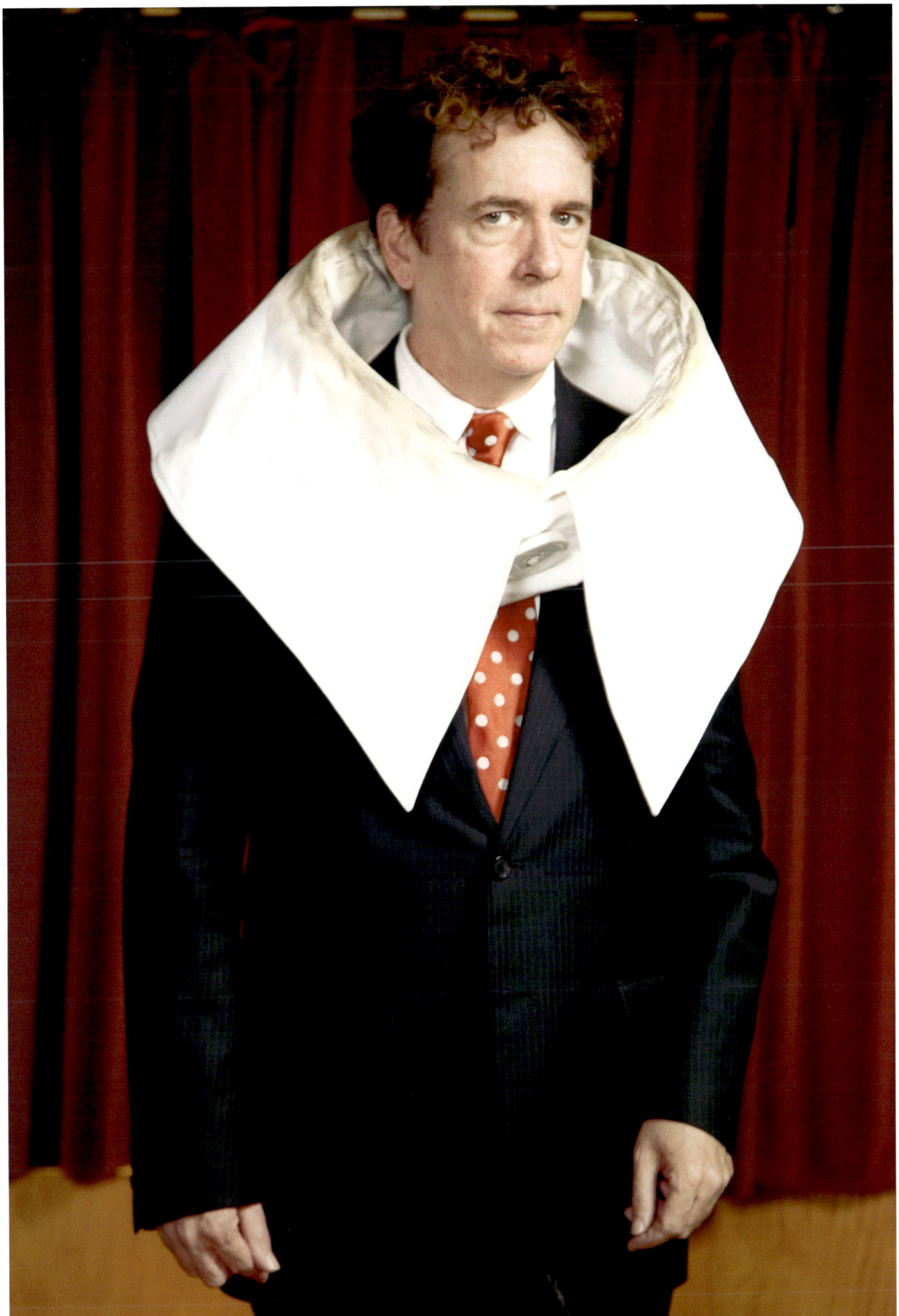

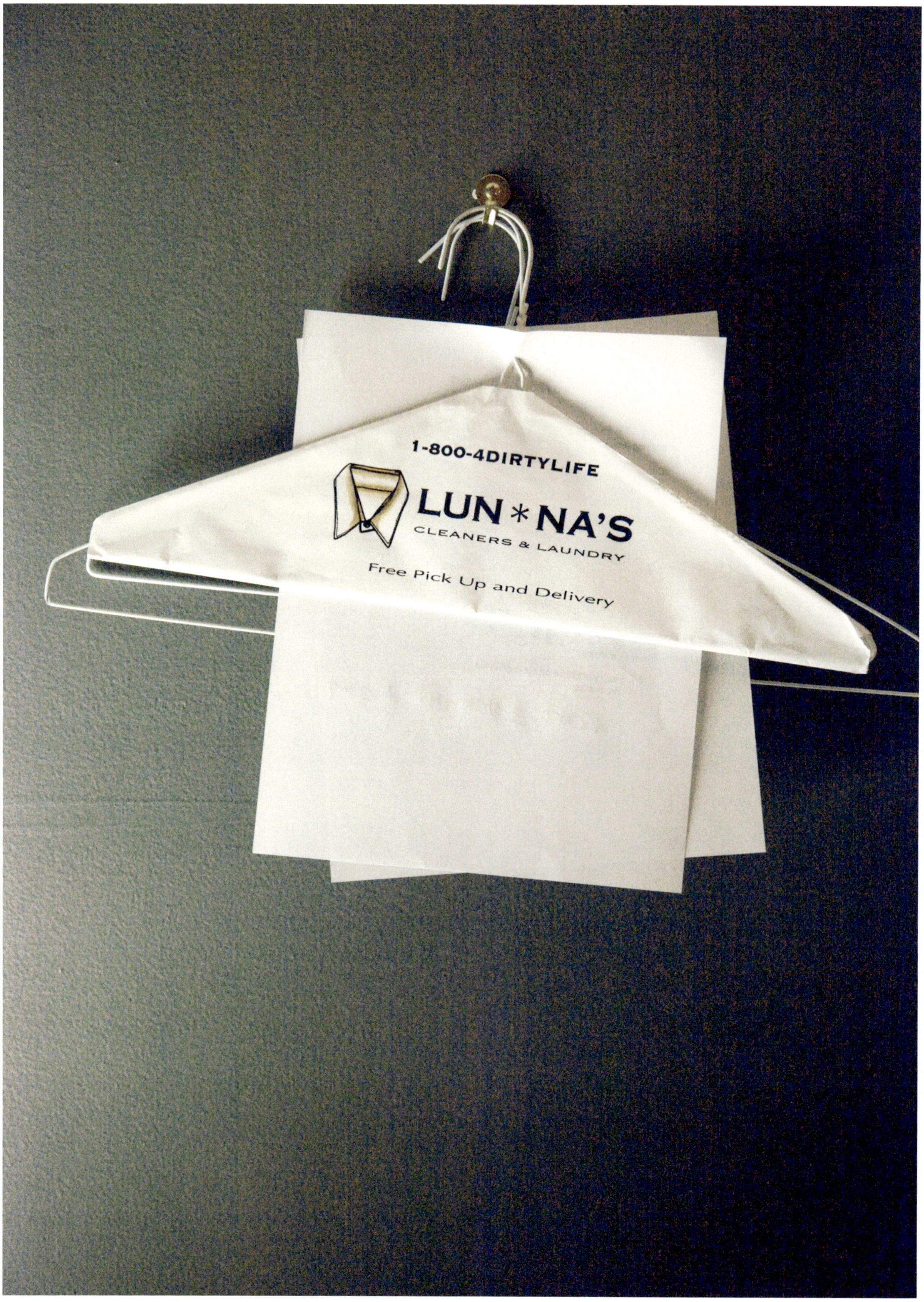
1-800-4DIRTYLIFE
LUN*NA'S
CLEANERS & LAUNDRY
Free Pick Up and Delivery

Afterword

When did I start collecting soiled white men's shirts? I think it was in the late 1990s. At the time, I frequented thrift stores and rag houses and was moved by the contrast between the formal, classic white shirts, which have basically remained unchanged for 100 years, and the very human and physical stains on their collars.
I was unaware of it then (as often happens), but there was a reason I was drawn to these shirts. The white shirt is a symbol for and a uniform of modern social structure, and the stains were evidence of white, rather than blue, collar manual labor. That evidence was something that had to be hidden from public view, and furthermore, it had historically been a woman's job to remove those same stains. There was even a catchy commercial nickname given to the stains: "ring around the collar."

I was intuitively driven to collect these rings around the collar. Once I began my collection, I made numerous intriguing discoveries. I felt as if I was collecting insects in the city. For one, there are infinite, if slight, variations in design between white shirts. I documented their various countries of production, their fabric content, and their labels. I also ranked them by how dirty they were. It was all fun.

At the time, I was still an amateur and collected every shirt I came across. I quickly amassed three hundred shirts. Without a place to archive them, I resorted to cutting off just the collars and saving them. I made fancy boxes for the collars I liked, and painted pictures of the collars I really liked. I noticed that with time, the stains lighten. I therefore devised a method of ironing them and burning the stain in before storing them. The stench this process produced was nauseating, so I took care to wear a mask and ventilate the room I was ironing in. Even with such precautions, I would sometimes have heartburn for days after long periods of ironing.

Soon enough, I had 500 shirts. Finally, I started to wonder what I was doing with them. I came up with the idea of recycling the dirty collars, making patchwork clothes out of them, and having a fashion show. This was in 2001. I also gave a slide show to explain the clothes. Naturally, the finale of the show was a wedding dress made of dirty collars.

I wanted to sell the clothes I had made, but no store would take the pieces, which were not only soiled, but also smelly. No one wanted to get married in the wedding dress either. I did find a sympathetic boutique, which displayed five or six pieces. Unfortunately, these pieces were stolen. Did the culprit think that these collars would make them money? Perhaps the thief was an olfactophiliac? I'm still puzzled as to what exactly happened.

A few years later I was invited to the Norwich Gallery in England to show the wedding dress and other pieces. I also exhibited pieces in a group show at the San Francisco Museum of Craft and Design. I then received a grant from the Peter S. Reed Foundation, which gave me the encouragement and means I needed to continue the dirty collars project.

In 2006, I organized a second "dirty collars" fashion show. By this time, I'd become quite picky in my collecting. I was now after rarity rather than quantity.
I exclusively collected dirty collars of designer shirts, which are a rare find. Unlike the first show, I therefore painted pictures of the collars and printed the pictures onto t-shirts and jackets. Around this time, I also had a desire to combine my visual work with music. For the show's soundtrack, I made a noise composition by drawing a shirt collar in a music sequencing software. After that, I also sang songs inspired by dirty collars. As I made and played music, I started to think that musicians' collars must also have been dirty. As a result of this thought, I painted headless portraits of my favorite musicians with soiled collars.

Fast forward to 2012. I was able to acquire a massive quantity of shirts for the exhibition I participated in at the Saitama Prefectural Modern Art Museum. This time, I made furniture covered in the collars, which I arranged as a room. I changed the layout of the room daily during the exhibition, and on the last day, I organized the furniture pieces in a line and slept on the bed.

In 2013, at the Velaslavasay Panorama, I performed a piece in which I surgically removed a part of a collar of a shirt brought in by a participant and sewed a label onto the shirt as proof of the removal. I also showed previously produced collar paintings and sculptures at the Panorama gallery's "Effulgence of the North."

Writing out the history of the project, I feel both that I've done a lot and that the project is chaotic and endless. I wonder when it will end. One thing is for sure-I do not see as many white shirts with soiled collars as I used to at thrift stores and used clothing stores. Rings around the collar are in decline.

Is it because people have grown more concerned about hygiene? Or is it a reflection of improvements in detergents and washing machines? Or do people throw out white shirts before they get soiled? The answer, probably, is all of the above.

The future will be white. Collars will be bleached and sterilized. White shirts will be kept white. And where will all the sweat and stains go? Perhaps in the future, rings around the collar will only manifest themselves in our minds.

Lun*na Menoh
March 2014
Translated by Taro Nettleton

List of Illustrations

Artist Biography

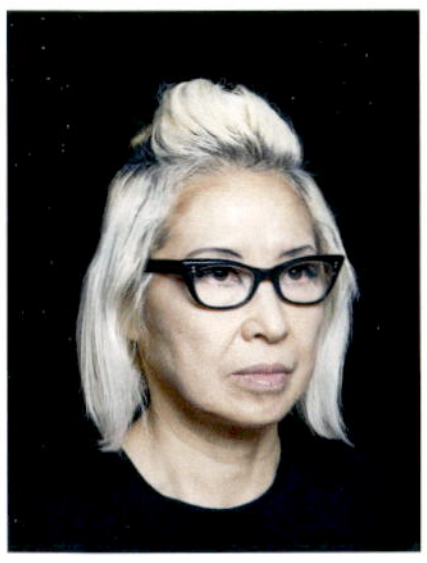

Born in Fukuoka, Japan, lives in Los Angeles
Joined electro pop band Seksu Roba (2000-2005)
Started bands Jean Paul Yamamoto (2005-) and Les Sewing Sisters (2010-)

SOLO EXHIBITIONS

2012 "C.A.J. duo exhibition with Adam Lee Miller" the Museum of Modern Art, Saitama, Japan
2010 "Ring Around the Collar/Musician" Track 16 Gallery, Santa Monica, CA, USA
2006 "Lun*na Menoh 1998-2006" Track 16 Gallery, Santa Monica, CA, USA
1994 "Boutique Mystique" Laguna Art Museum Satellite, Cossta Mesa, CA, USA

GROUP EXHIBITIONS

2013 "SUN OF A BEACH" Denis Brun Studio, Marseille, France
2006 "Queen of the Night" Berman/Turner project, Santa Monica, CA, USA
2005 "Nouvelle Nuptials New Visions in Wedding Traditions" The Museum of Craft and Design, San Francisco, CA, USA
"Twisted Christmas" BGH Gallery, Santa Monica, CA, USA
2004 "the Leopard Spots:Between Art, Performance and Club Culture" 18th Street Arts Center, Santa Monica, CA, USA
2001 "EAST international" Norwich University College of the Arts, Norwich, UK
1999 "Primordial/Soup to Nuts" Dirt Gallery, Los Angeles, CA, USA
1998 "Precious" Jan Baum, Los Angeles, CA, USA
"Addressing the Century-100 Years of Art & Fashion," Hayward Gallery, London, UK
1997 "Yard Sale" Special K Exhibition, Los Angeles, CA, USA
1996 "Lovers Labors Lost" Site Gallery, Los Angeles
1995 "Action Station Exploring Open Systems" Santa Monica Museum of Art, Santa Monica, CA, USA
"Felicity" Jan Baum, Los Angeles, CA, USA
1988 "Fashion & Surrealism" Victoria and Albert Museum, London, UK

PERFORMANCES

2012 art performance "Collar Surgery" the Velaslavasay Panorama, Los Angeles, CA, USA
2011 conceptual fashion show "Maximum Miniature" music by Les Sewing Sisters, Track 16 Gallery, Santa Monica, CA, USA
2009 conceptual fashion show "Headdress 2009" music by Les Sewing Sisters, Royal/T, Culver City, CA, USA
2008 conceptual fashion show "Couture Salvage" music by Jean Paul Yamamoto, Track 16 Gallery, Santa Monica, CA, USA
art performance "Improvising Sewing" music by Jean Paul Yamamoto, Royal/T, Culver City, CA, USA
2006 art performance "Re Cut" Los Angeles Contemporary Exhibitions, music by Jean Paul Yamamoto, Los Angeles, CA, USA
conceptual fashion show "Ring Around the Collar" music by Jean Paul Yamamoto, Track 16 Gallery, Santa Monica, CA, USA
2005 Seksu Roba performed at Santa Barbara Museum of Art, Santa Barbara, CA, USA
2004 Seksu Roba performed "Side Street Project" Los Angeles County Museum of Art, Los Angeles, CA, USA
2003 group performance "Andy Warhol Retrospective" The Museum of Contemporary Art, Los Angeles, CA, USA
2001 conceptual fashion show "Ring Around the Neck" ARC Studio, Los Angeles, CA, USA
1998 conceptual fashion show "Spring-Summer 1770-1998" Art Share, Los Angeles, CA, USA
1997 conceptual fashion show "He(ad)dress" Jan Baum, Los Angeles, CA, USA
1992 conceptual fashion show "Dress for Poet" Beyond Baroque, Venice, CA, USA

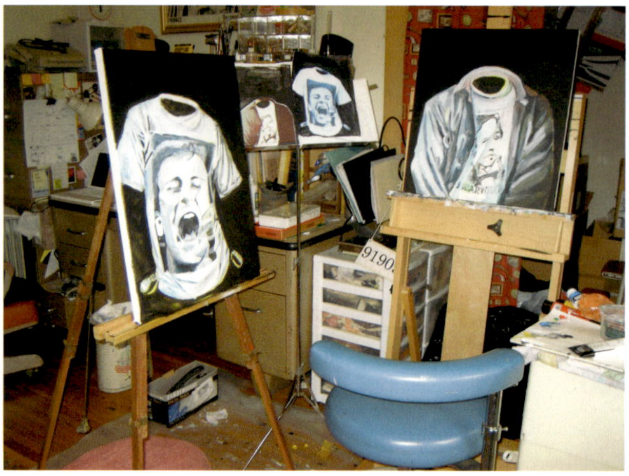

Proofreading and Editing: Manuel Chavarria

Production Assistants: Moeko Maeda, Natsuki Mitunaka, Takuya Ichinose, Saori Mitome, Taeko Ishibiki

Very special thanks to:

Ichiro Shimizu, Lulu, Track 16, Kristine Mckenna, Yuichi and Ikuko Shimada, Koji Iijima
Atsushi Yazaki, Adam Lee Miller, Nicola Kuperus, Ruth Bernstein, Katerina Alexy, Benjamin Kidwell Lein
Emmi Joutsi, Vanessa Gonzalez, Sterling Andrews, Audrey Wollen, Andrew L.Hanson, Felipe Sanchez
Lance Rock, Christopher Curtis, Brian Gottliieb, Matt Johnstone, Troy Haling, Ashley Kennedy
Kemba Russell, Percephenie, Sara Velas, Jade Finlinson, Ruby and XYZ club, Makkie Asako, , Dai-cyan
Tricia Gabriel, Mike Slack, Reiko Kondo, Yuko Takahashi, Nikki Fosmore Thewes, Relah Eckstein
Tsugumi Takashi, Avery Brooks, Yukiko Nakashima, Rie Fujii, Mike Penny, Alan Myers